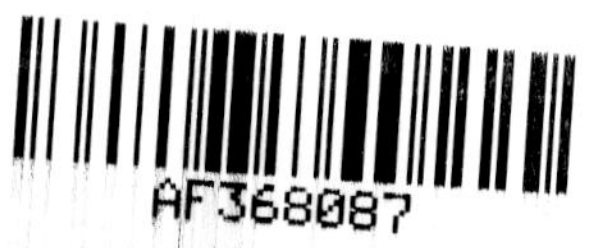

Bunny, Eggs

GIRLS
AND FRIENDS

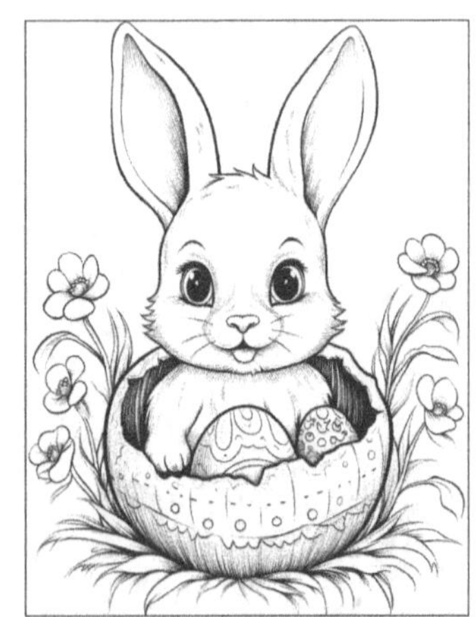 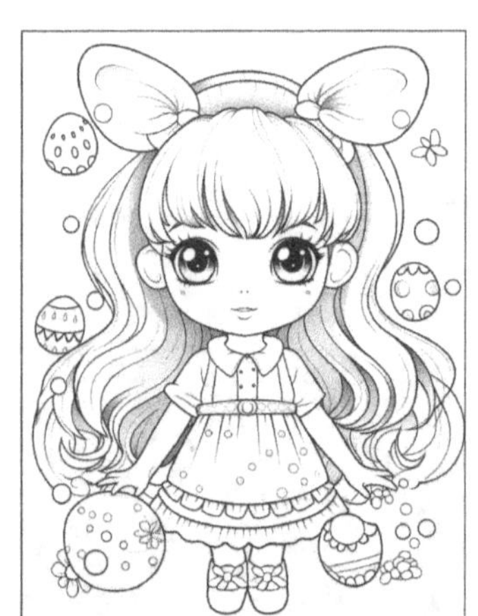 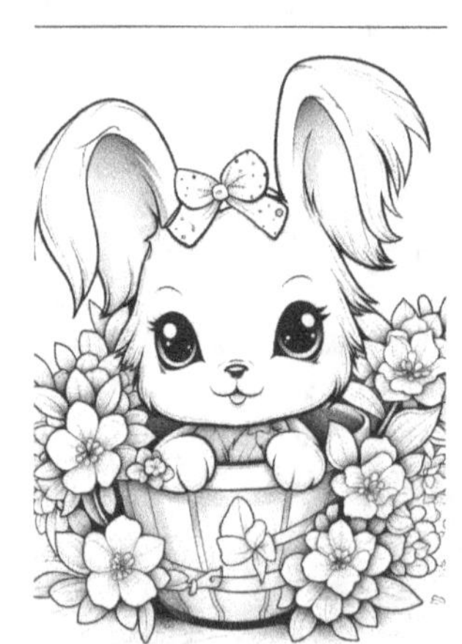

This book Belong to

____

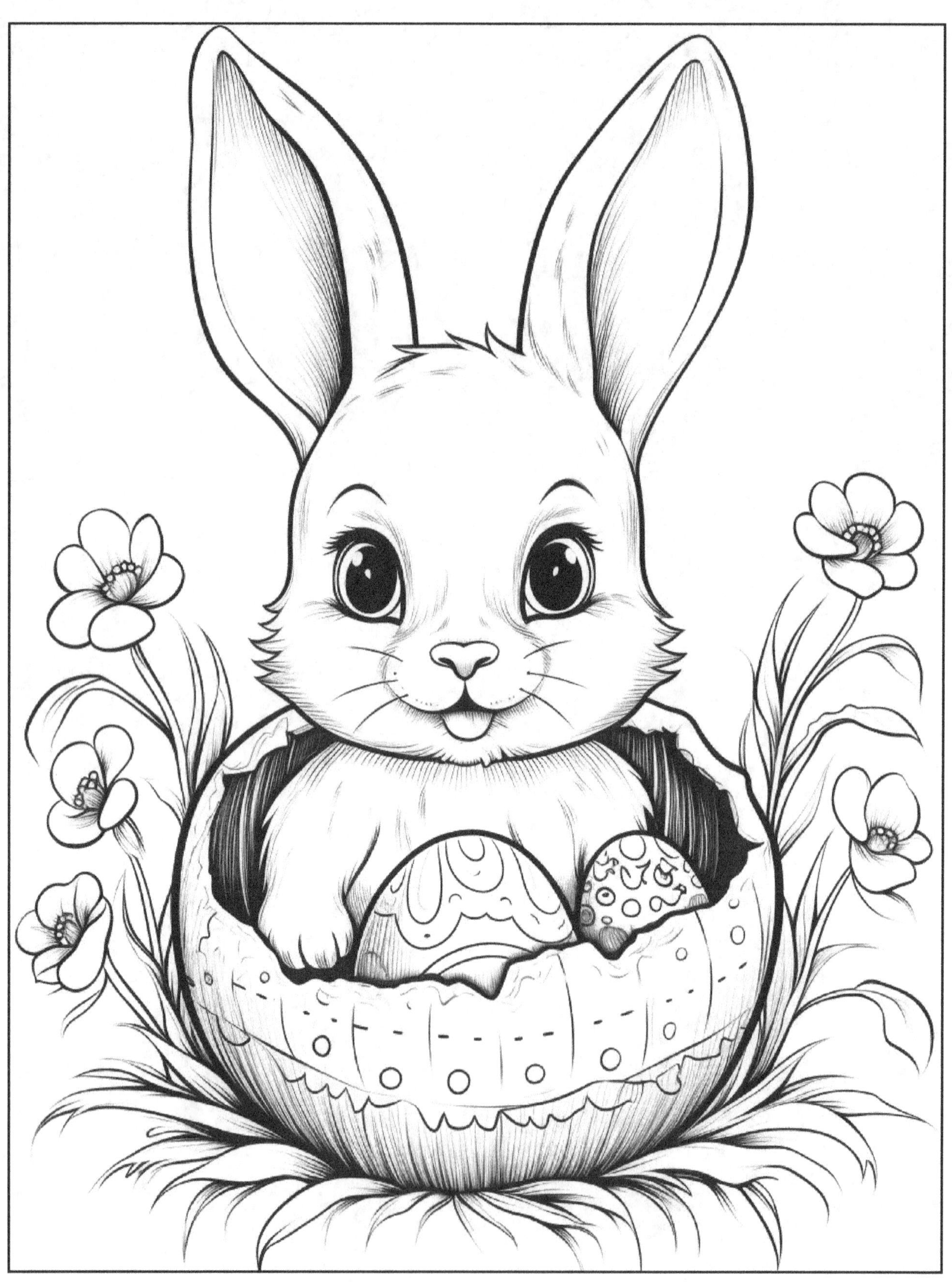

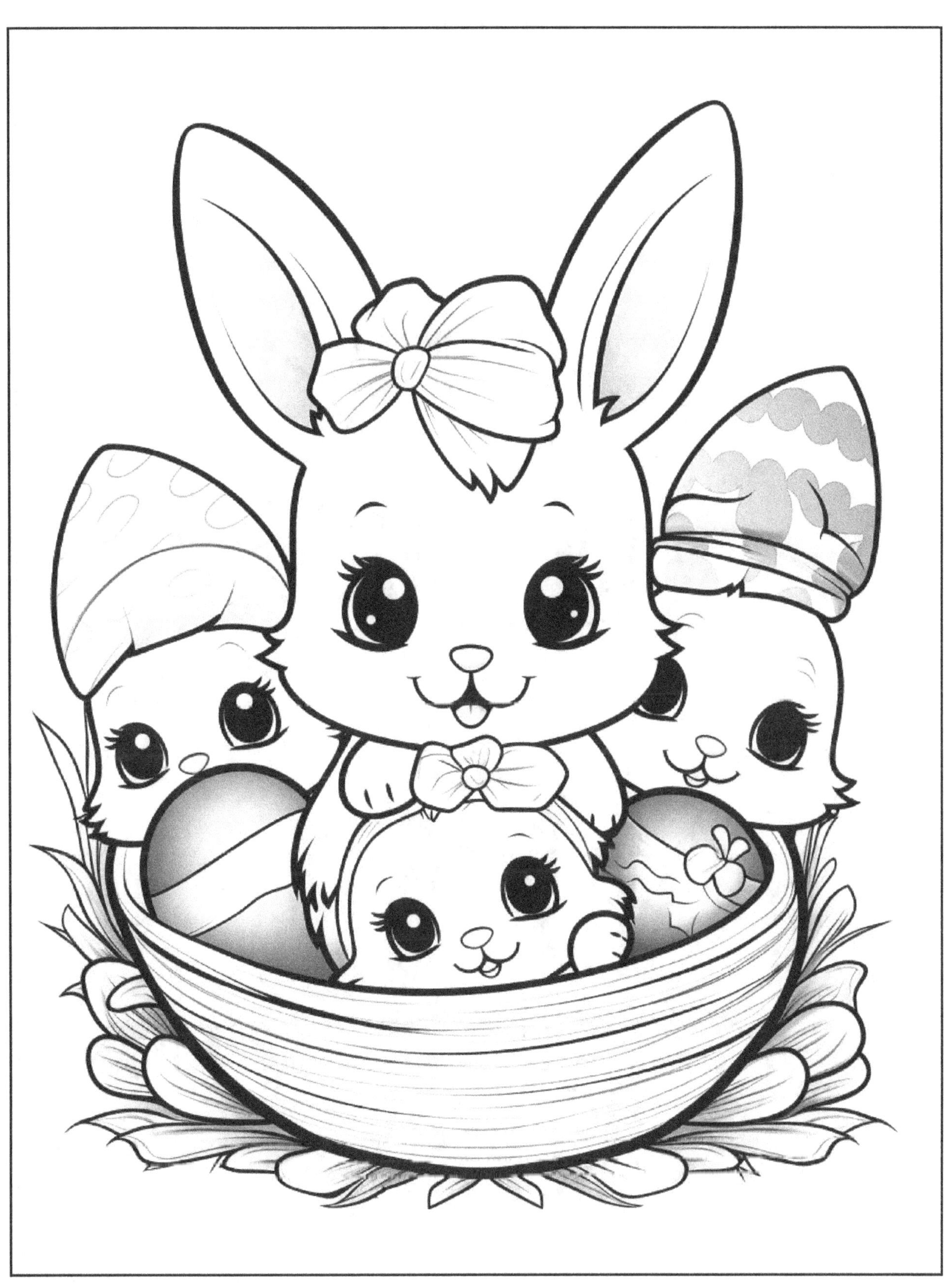

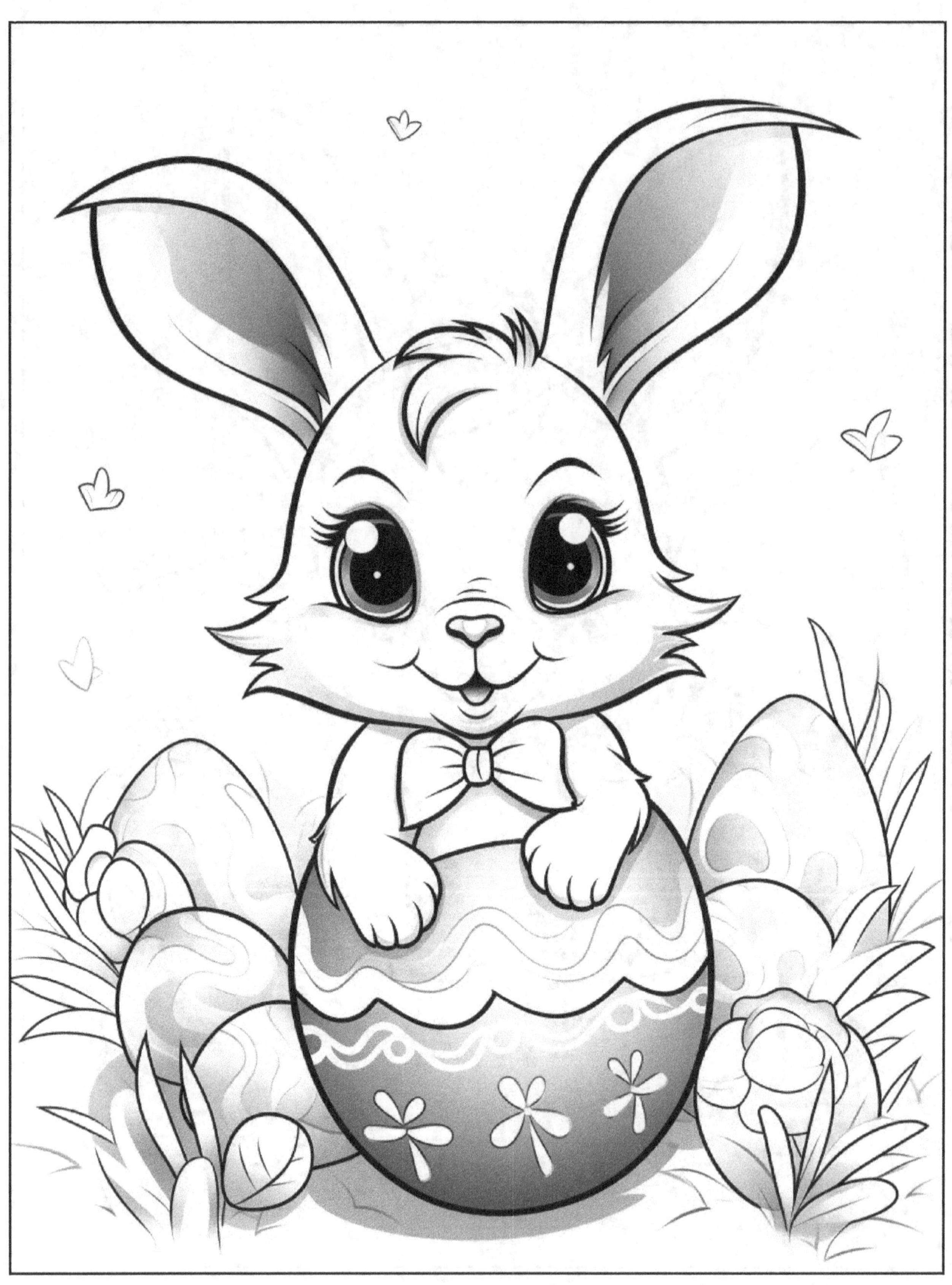

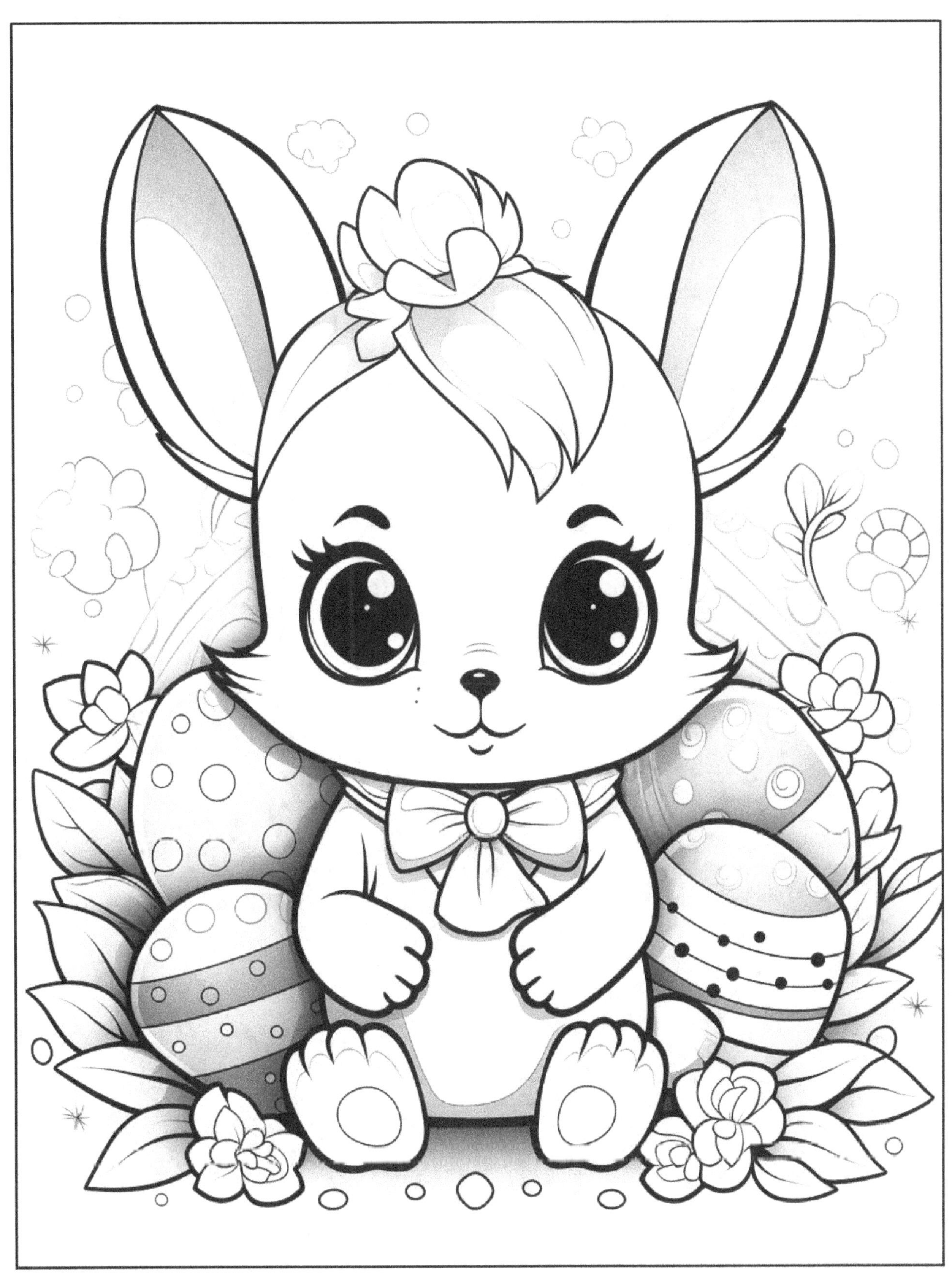

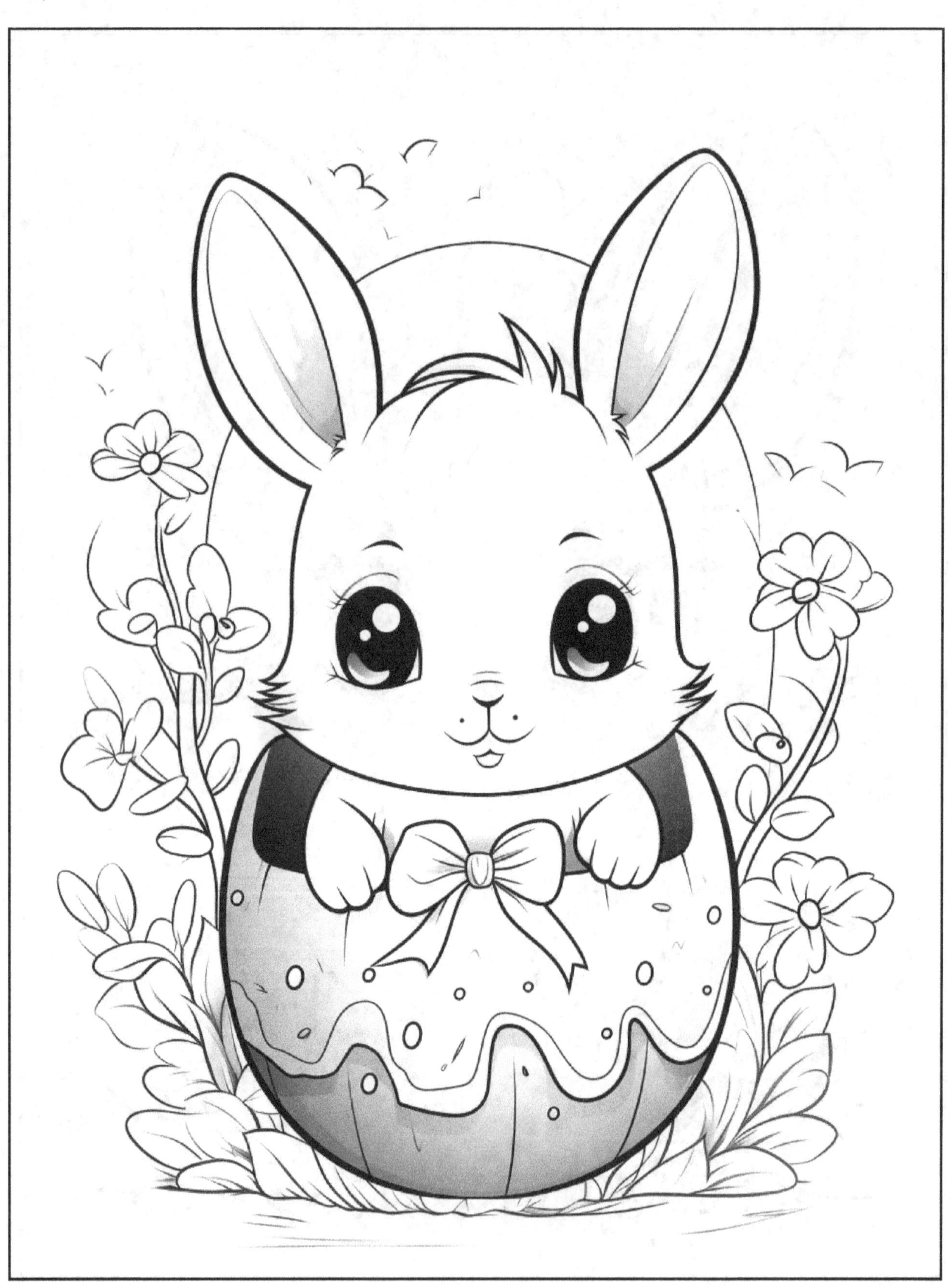

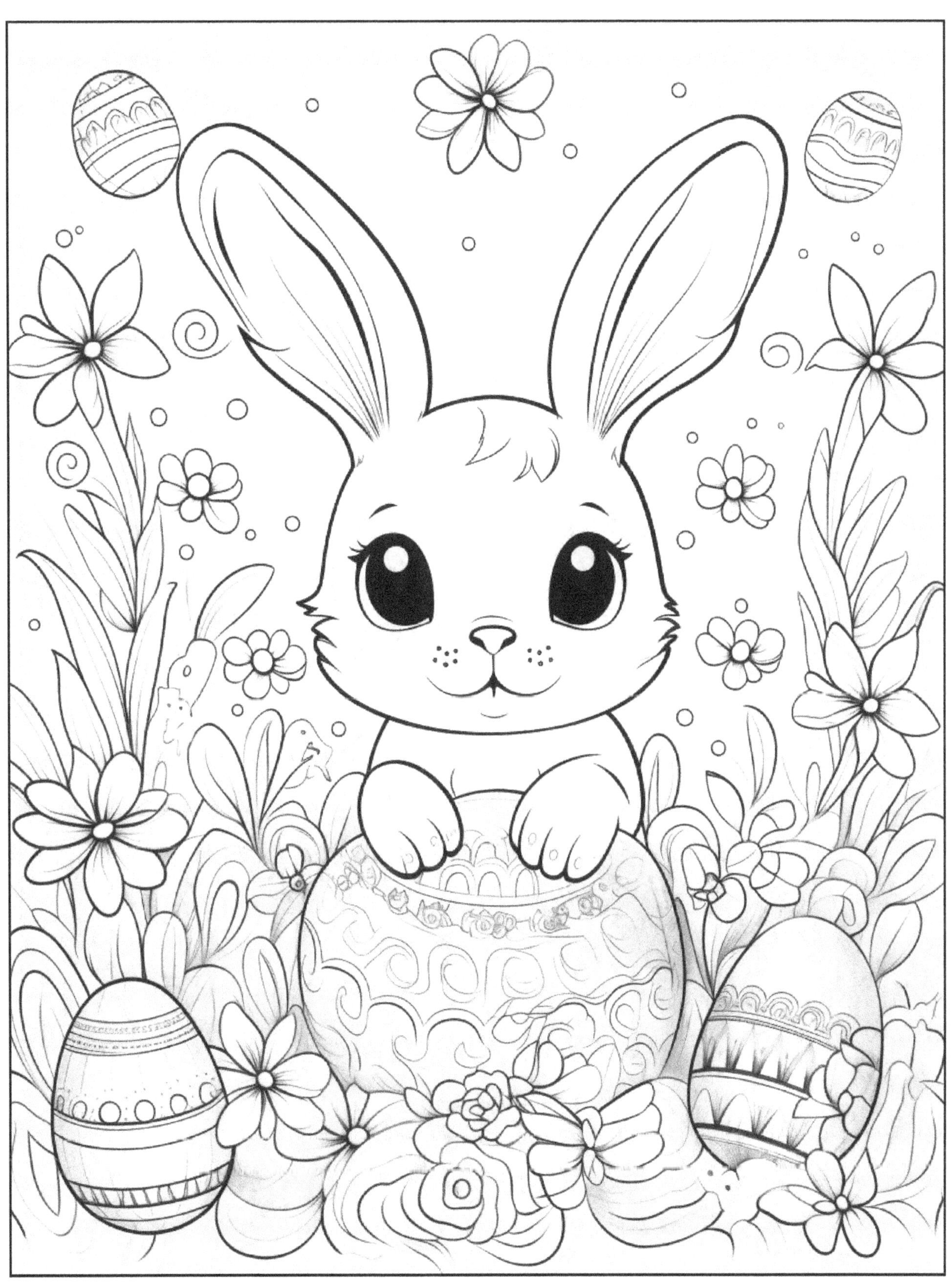

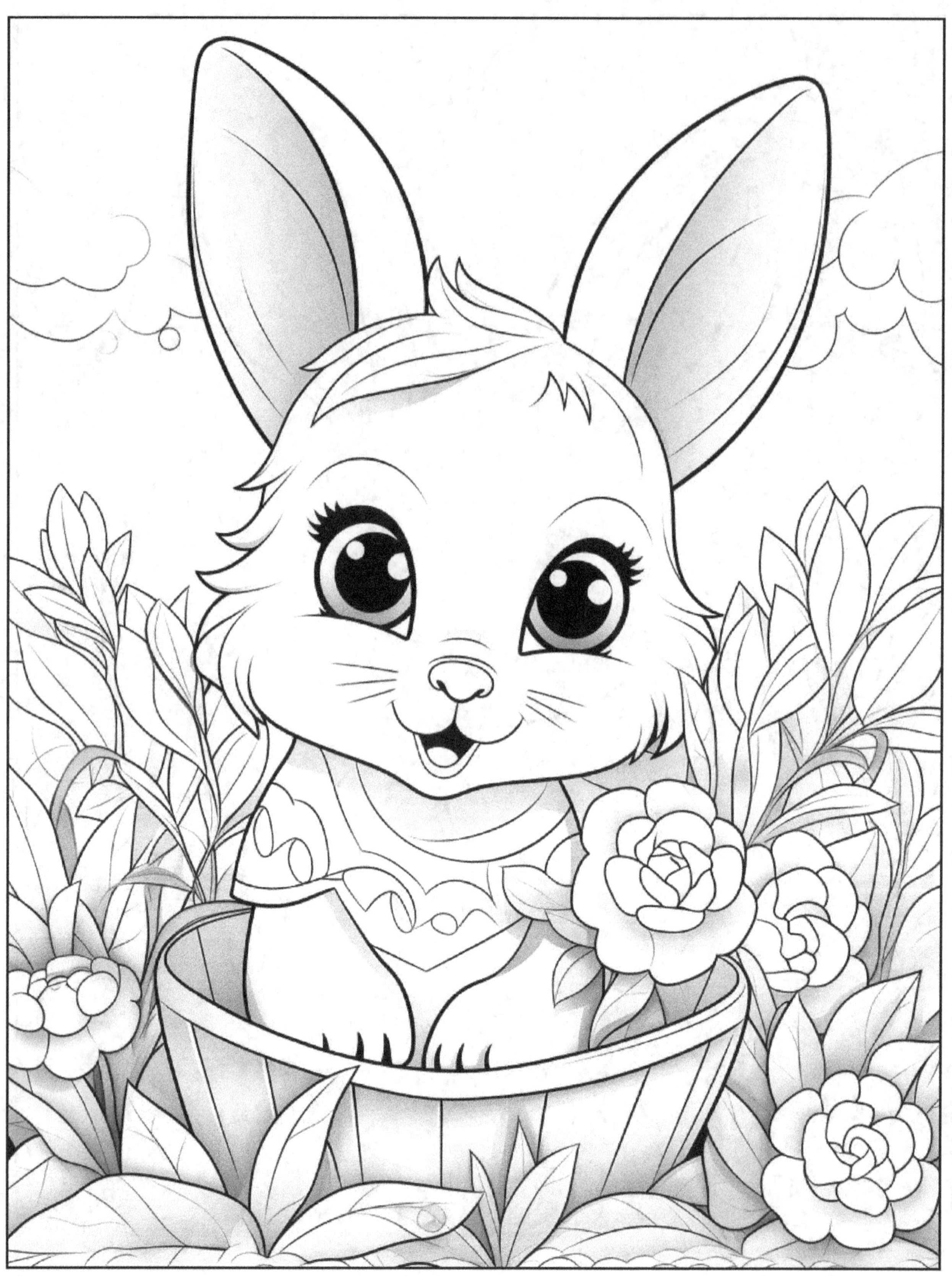

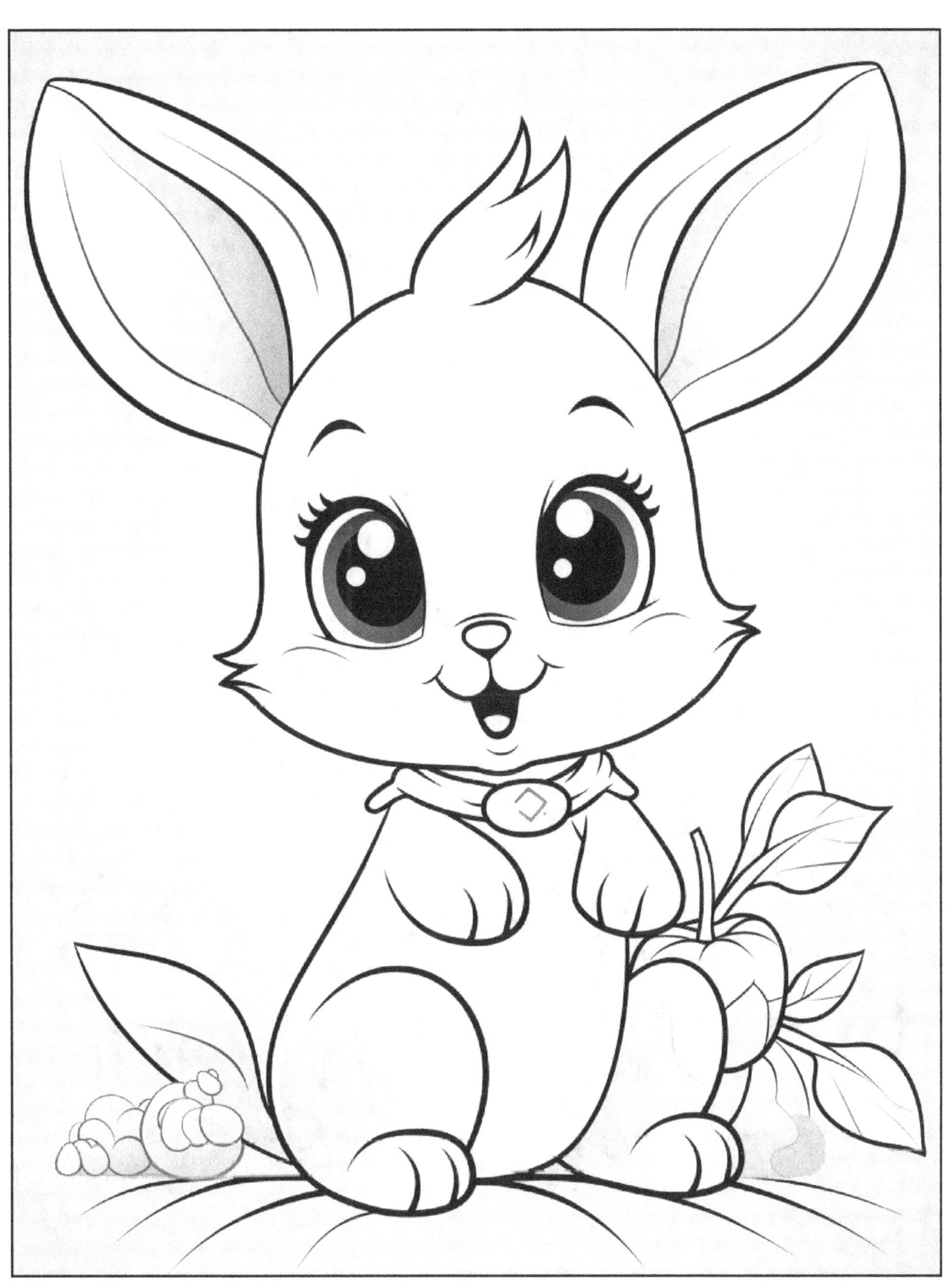

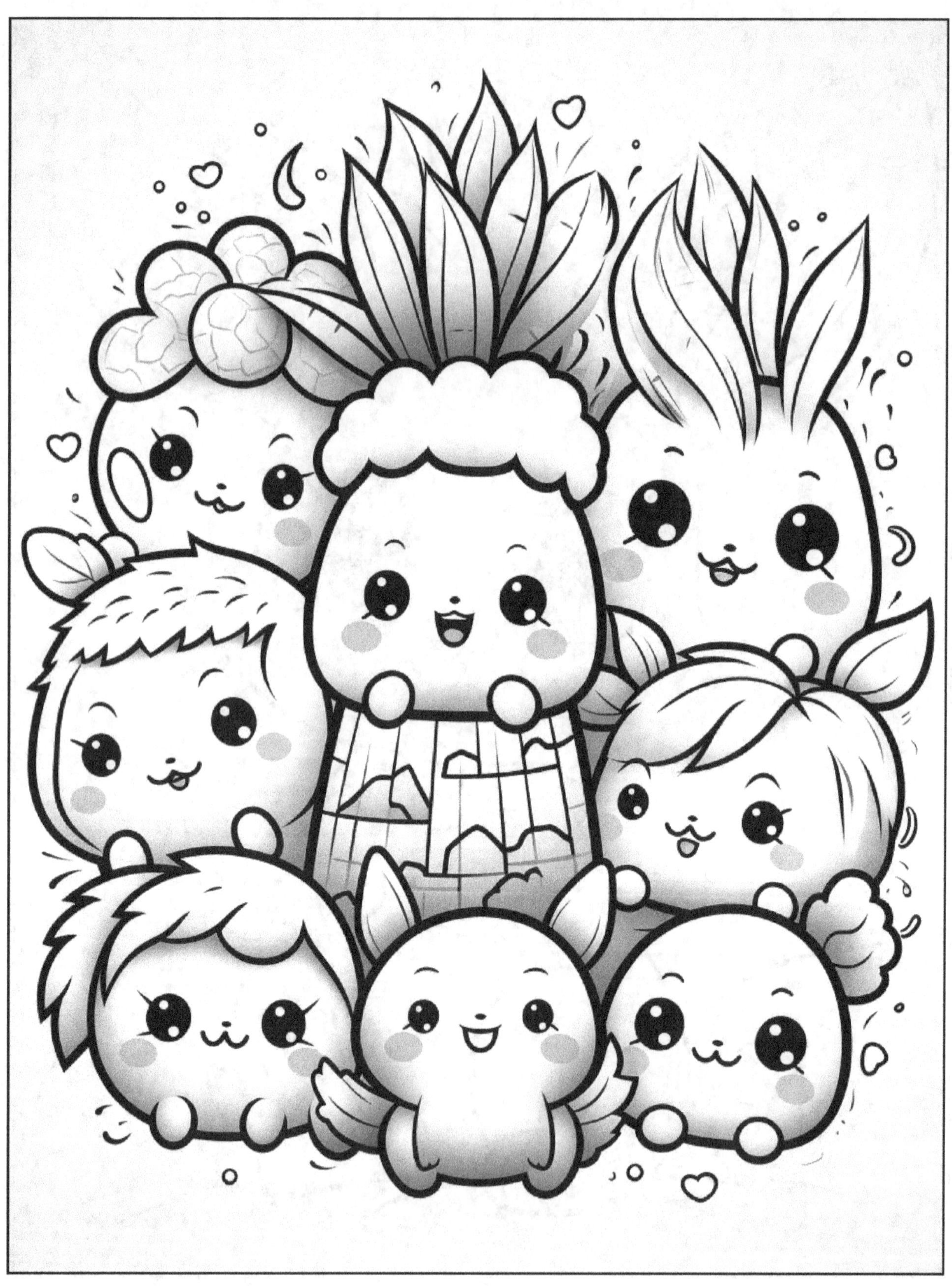

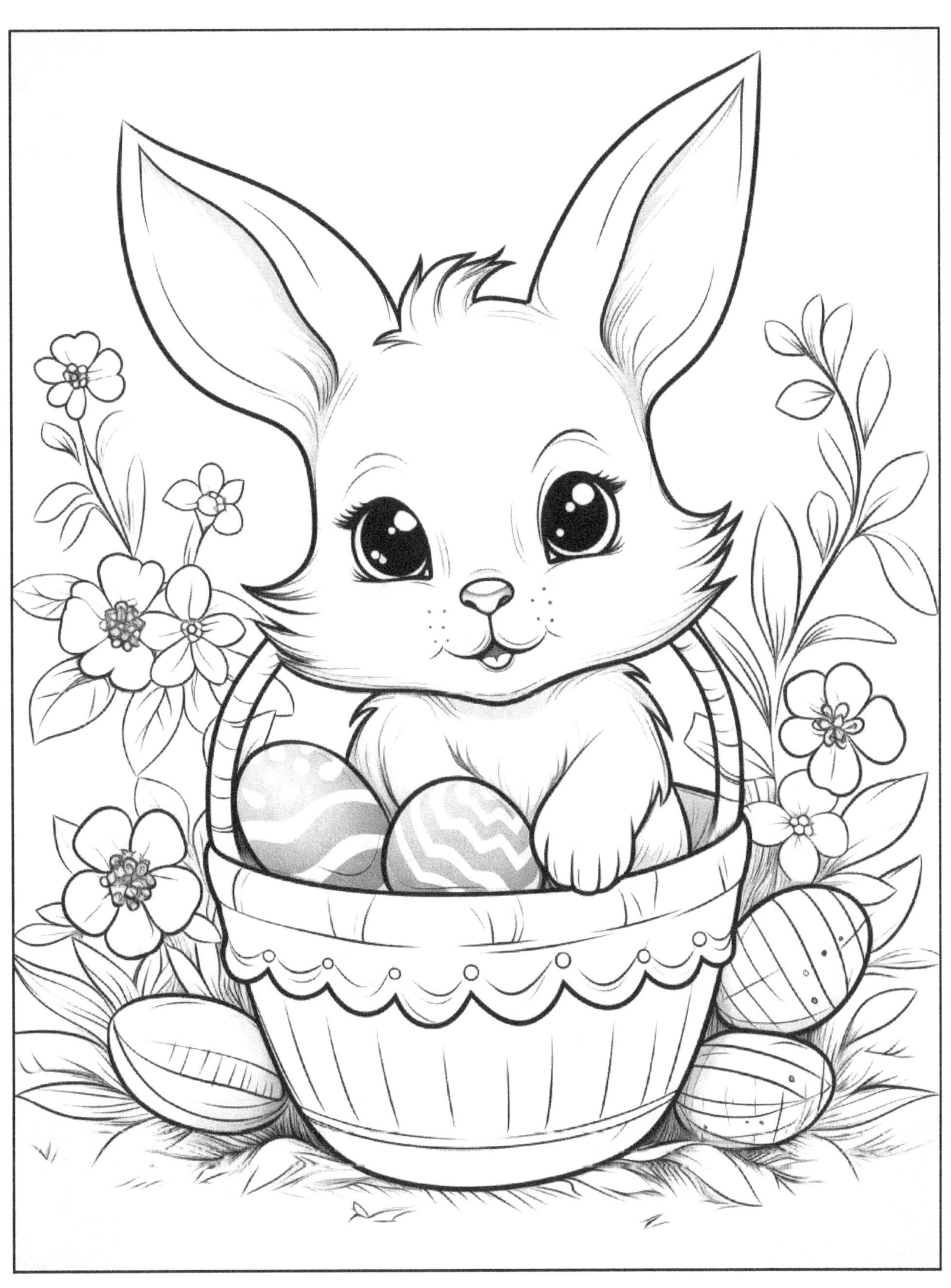

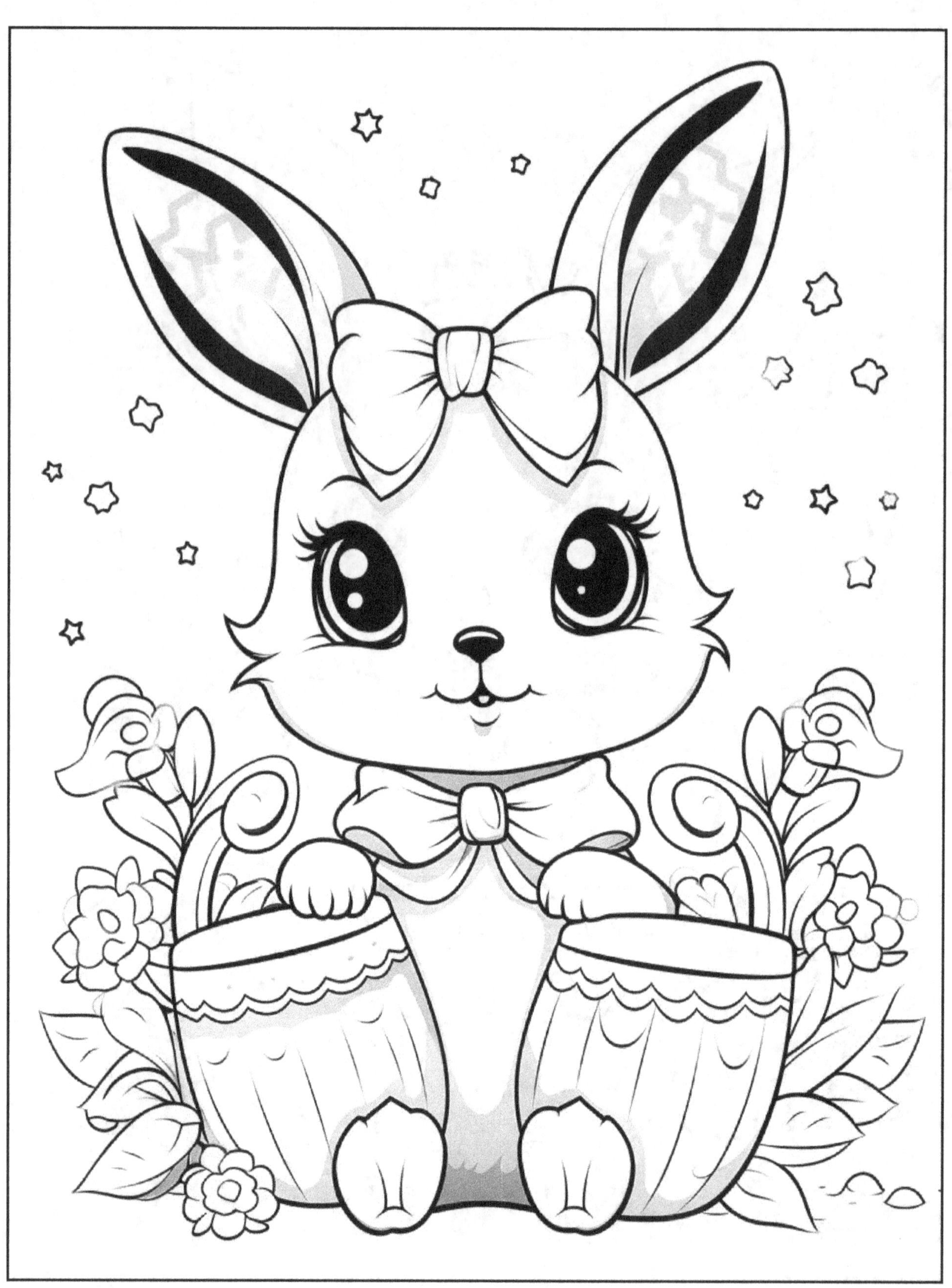

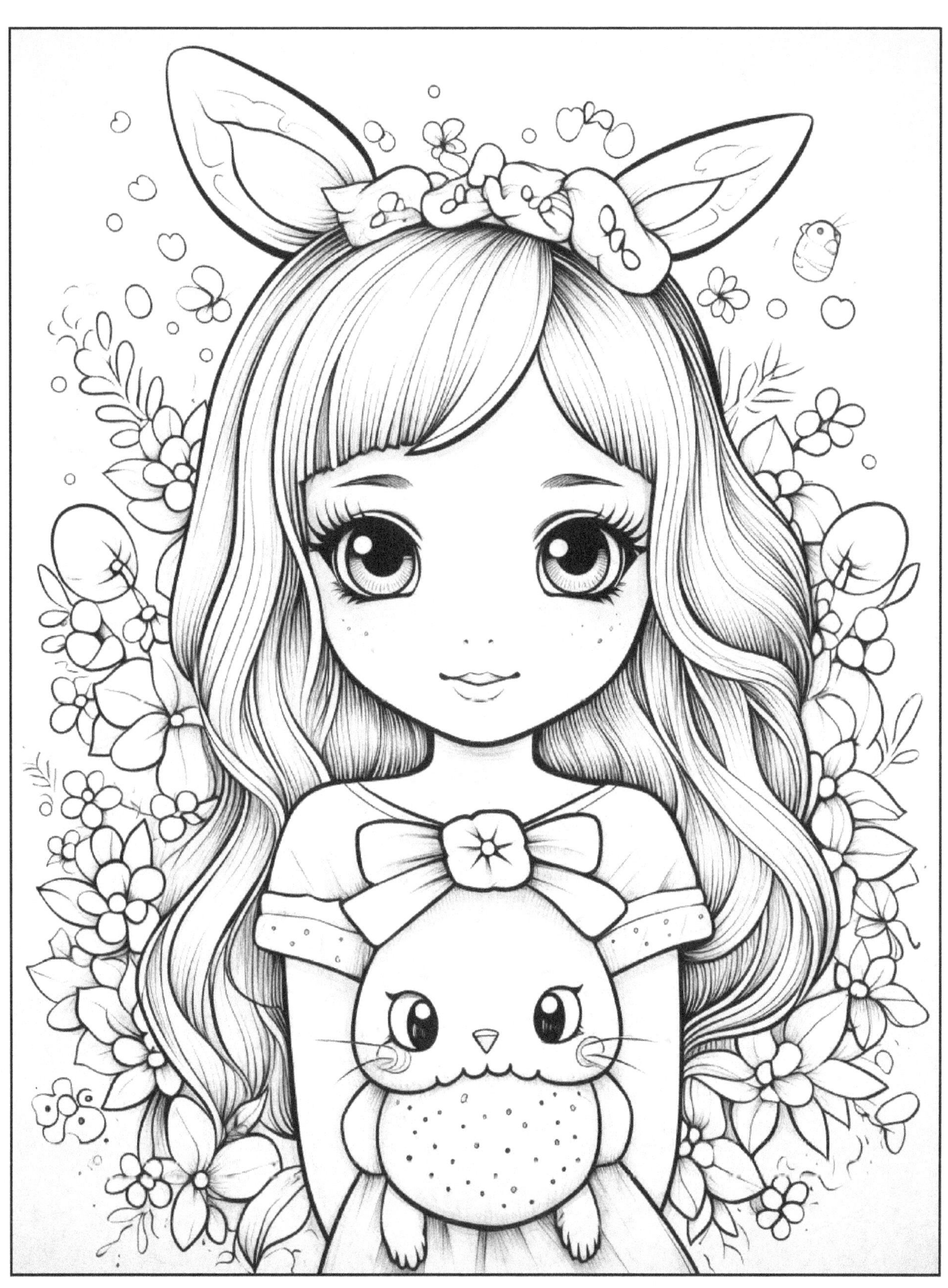

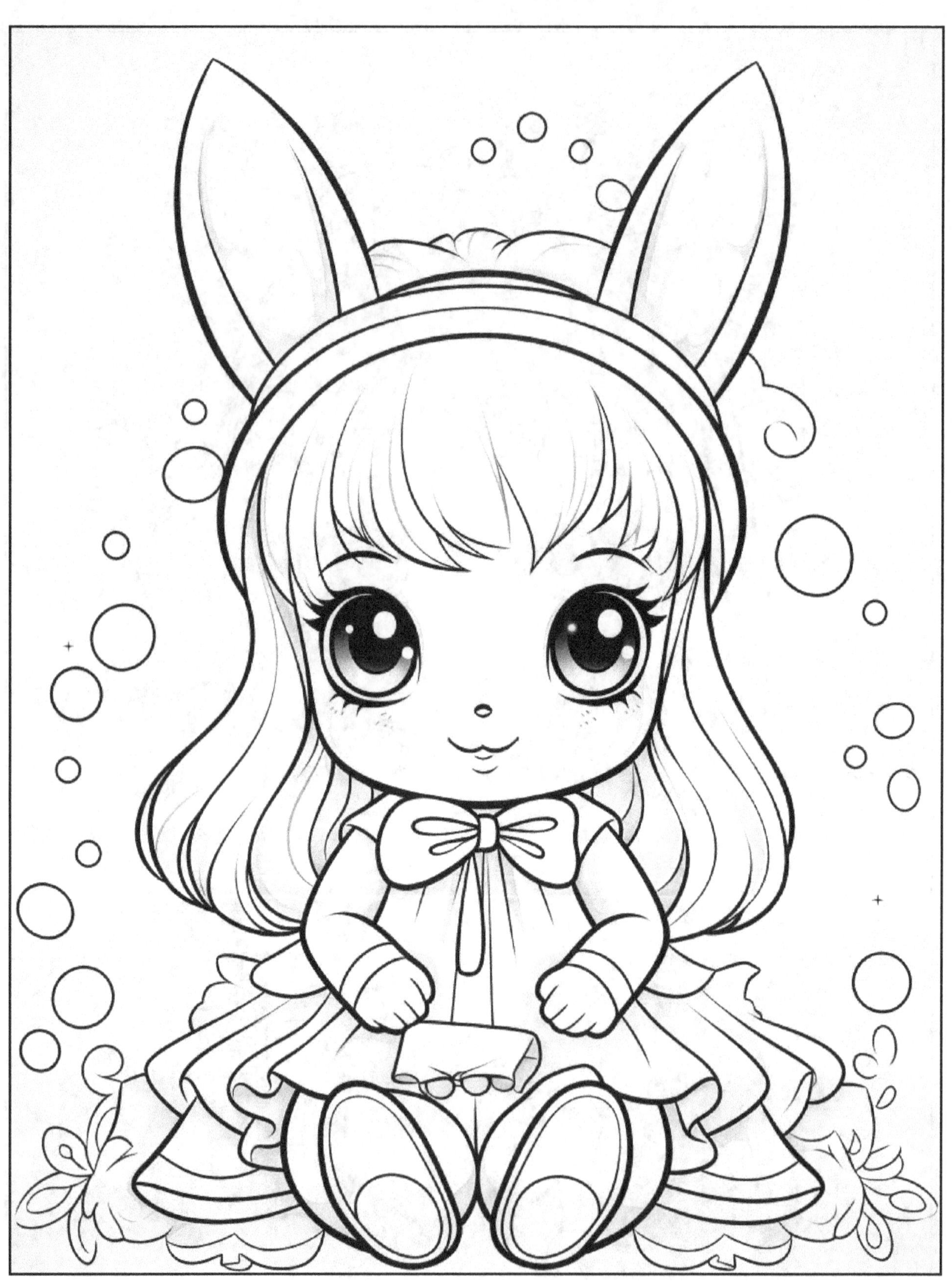

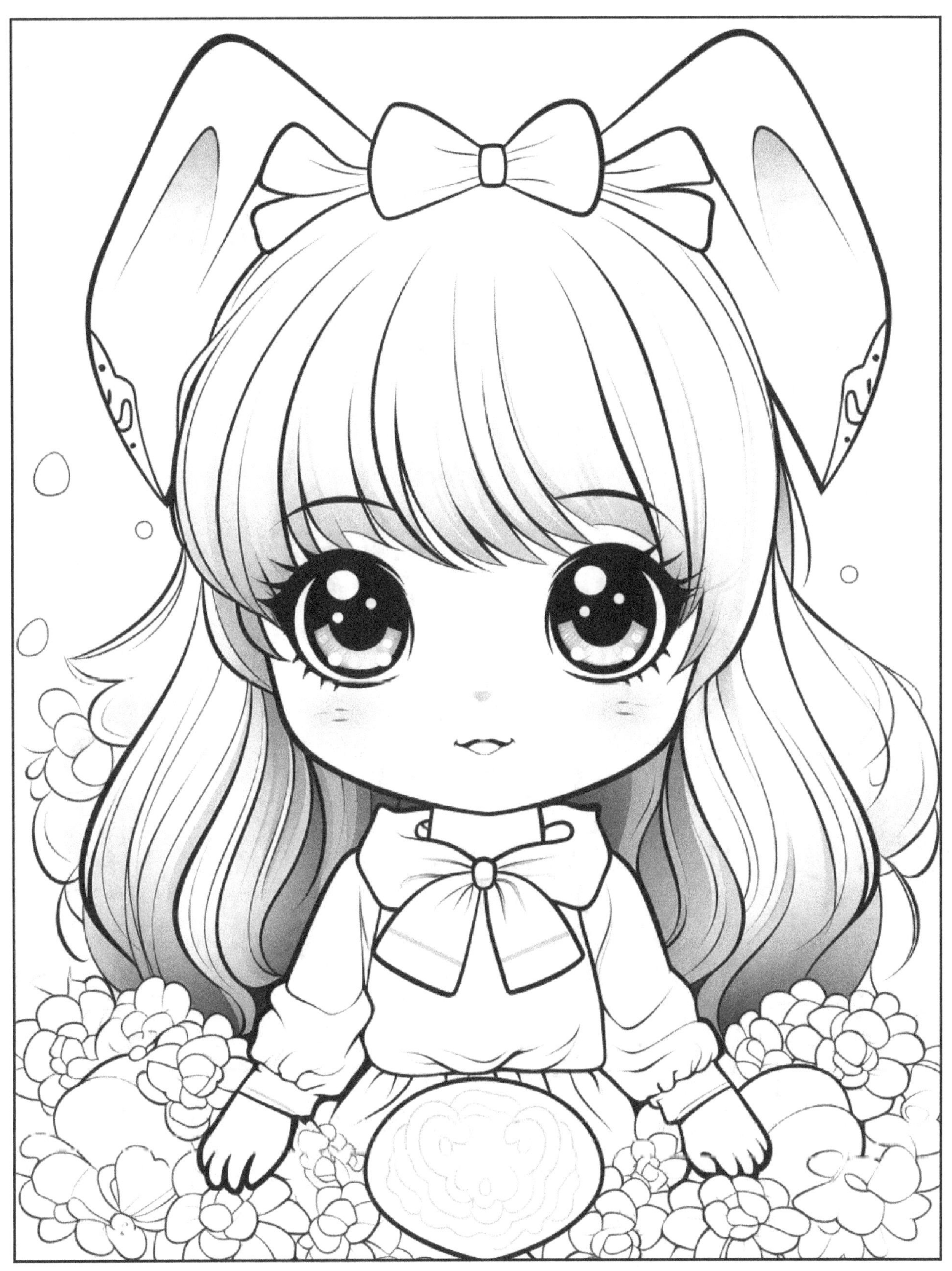

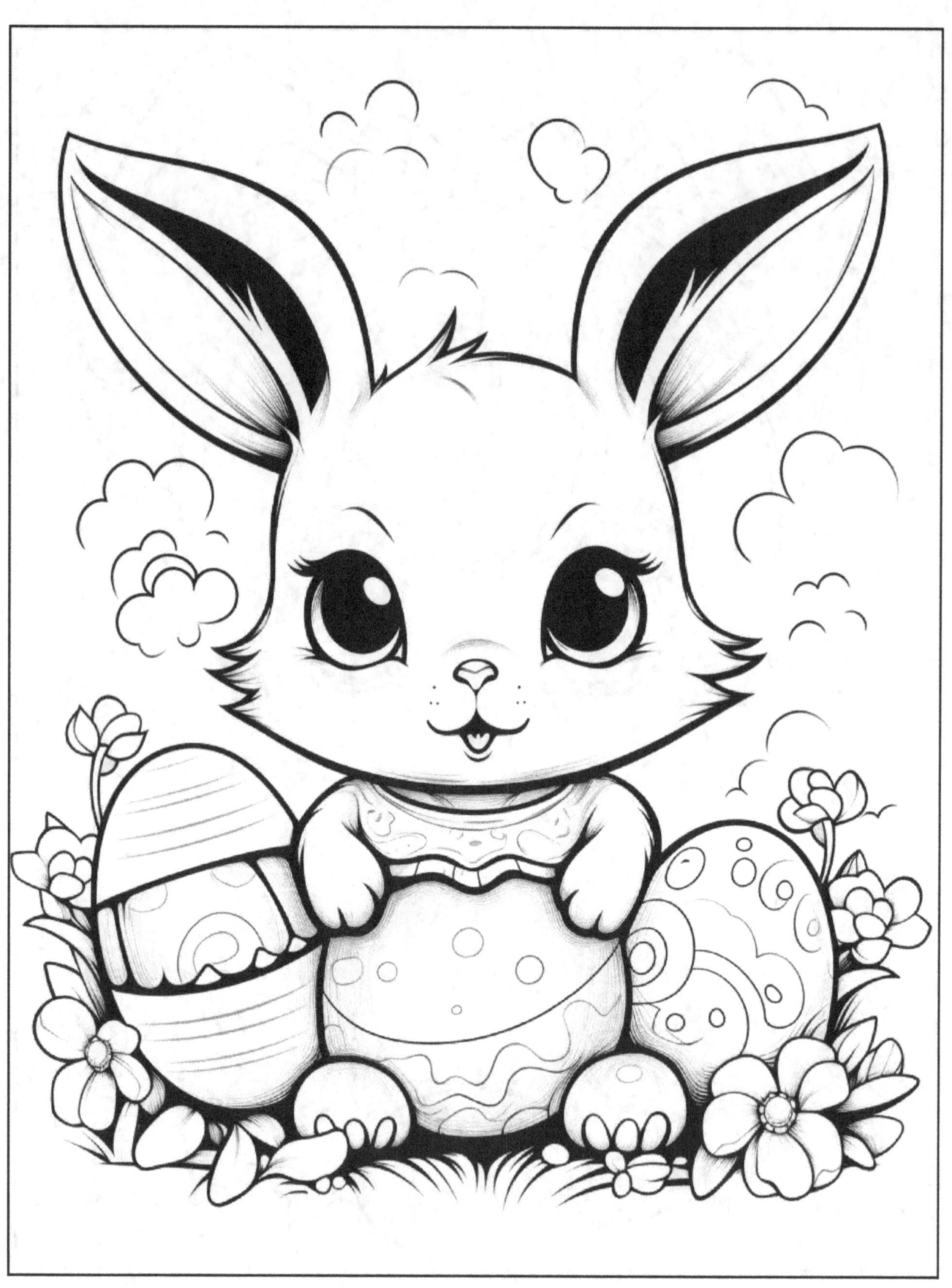

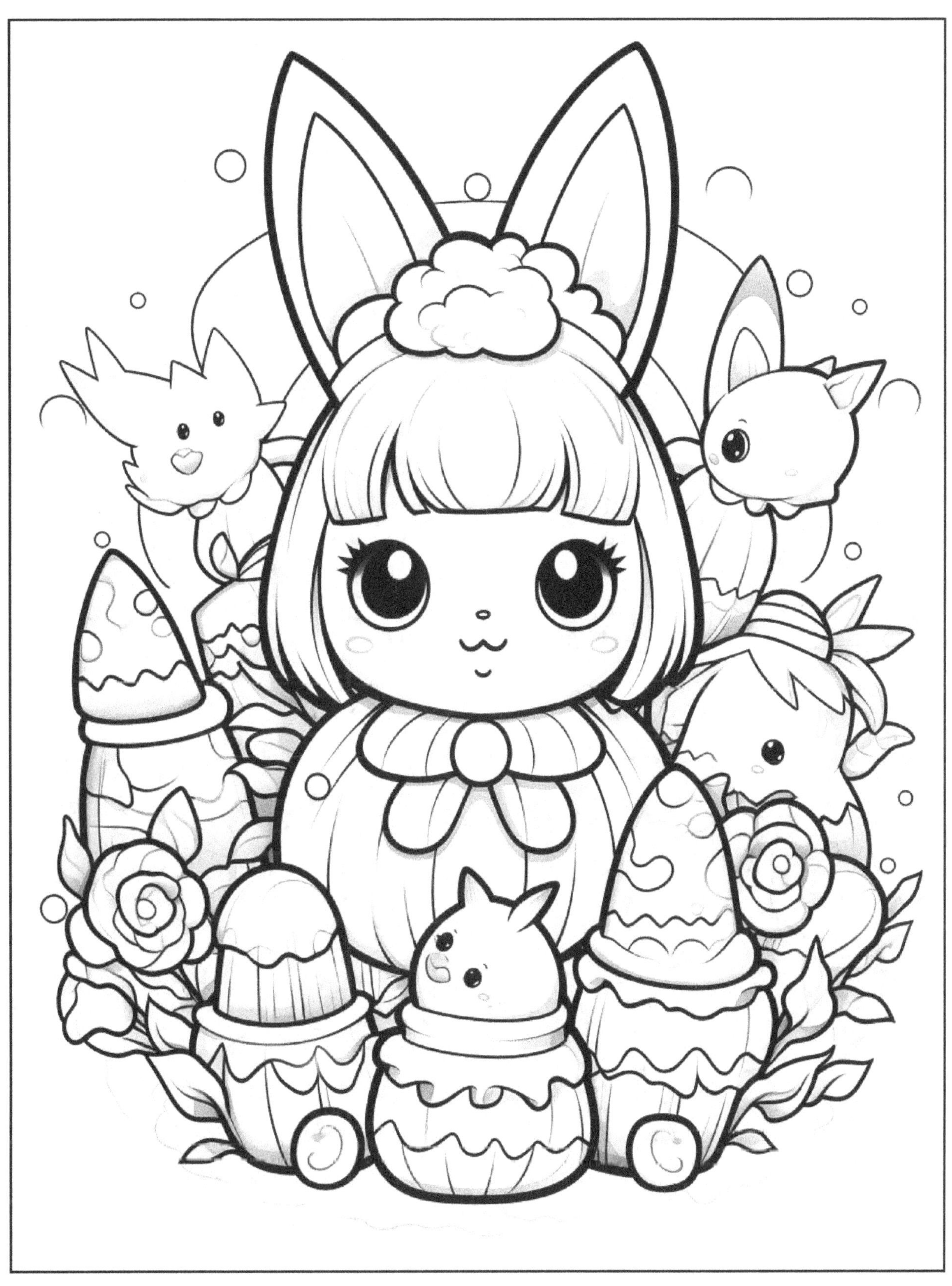

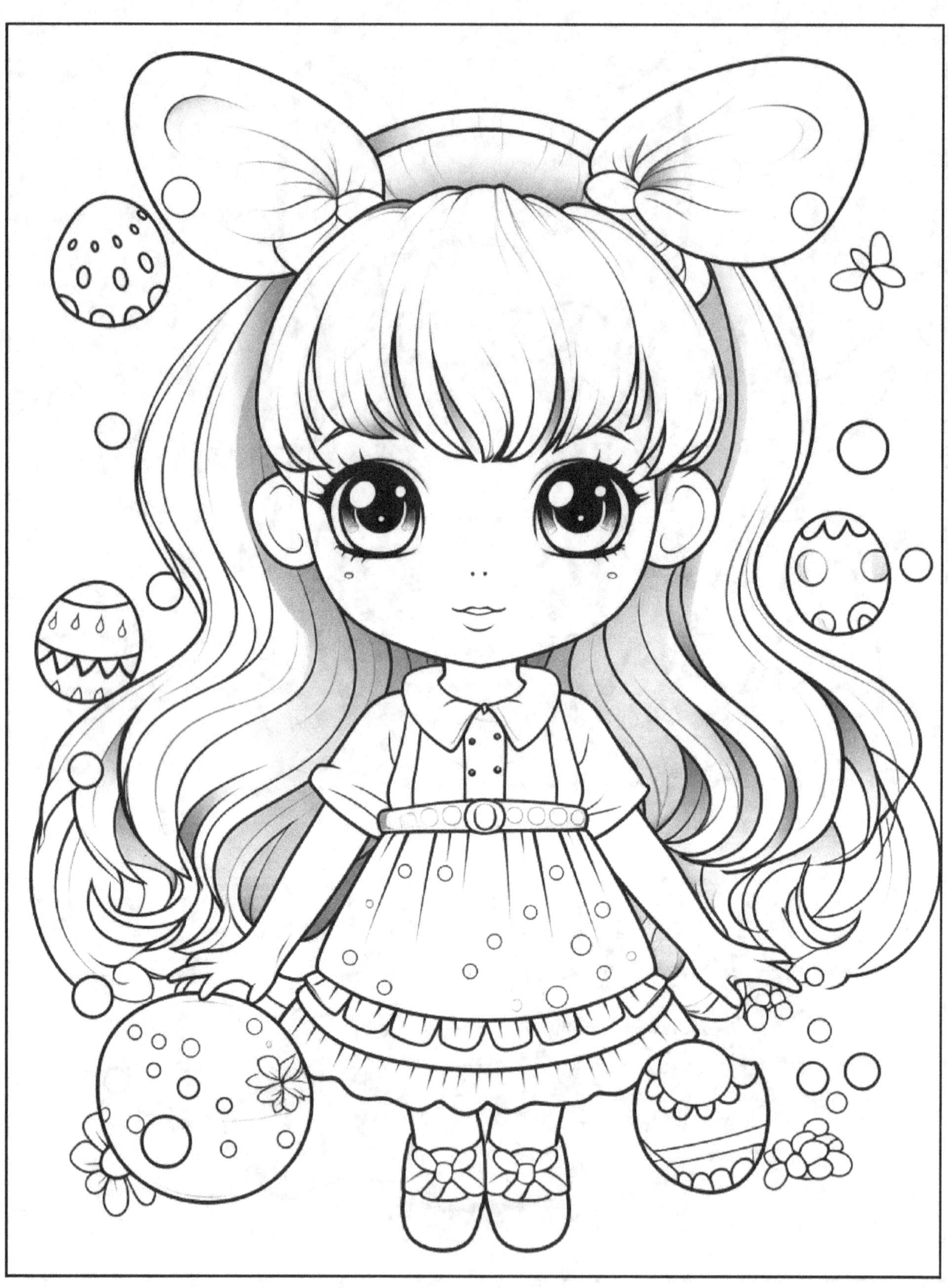

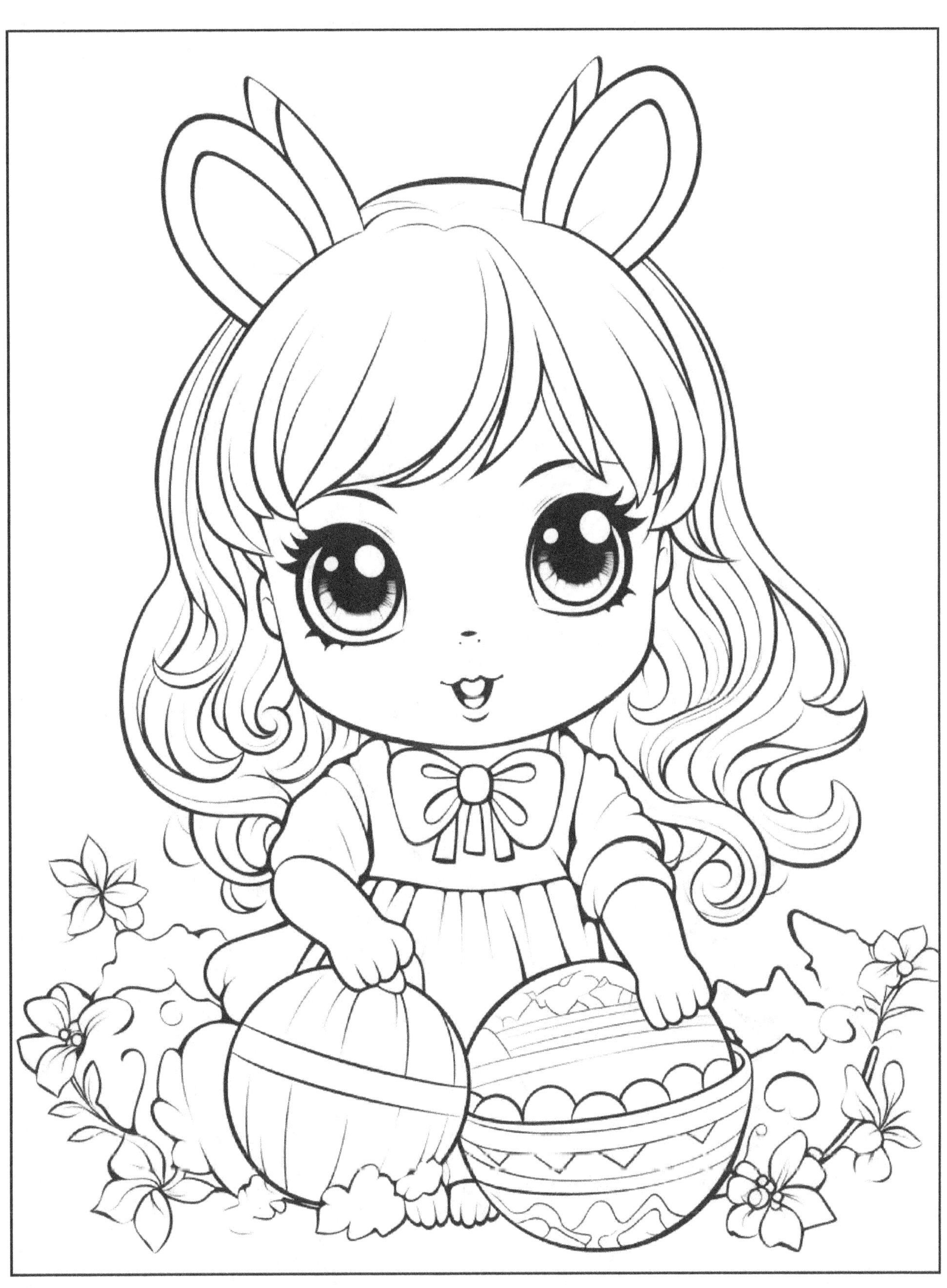

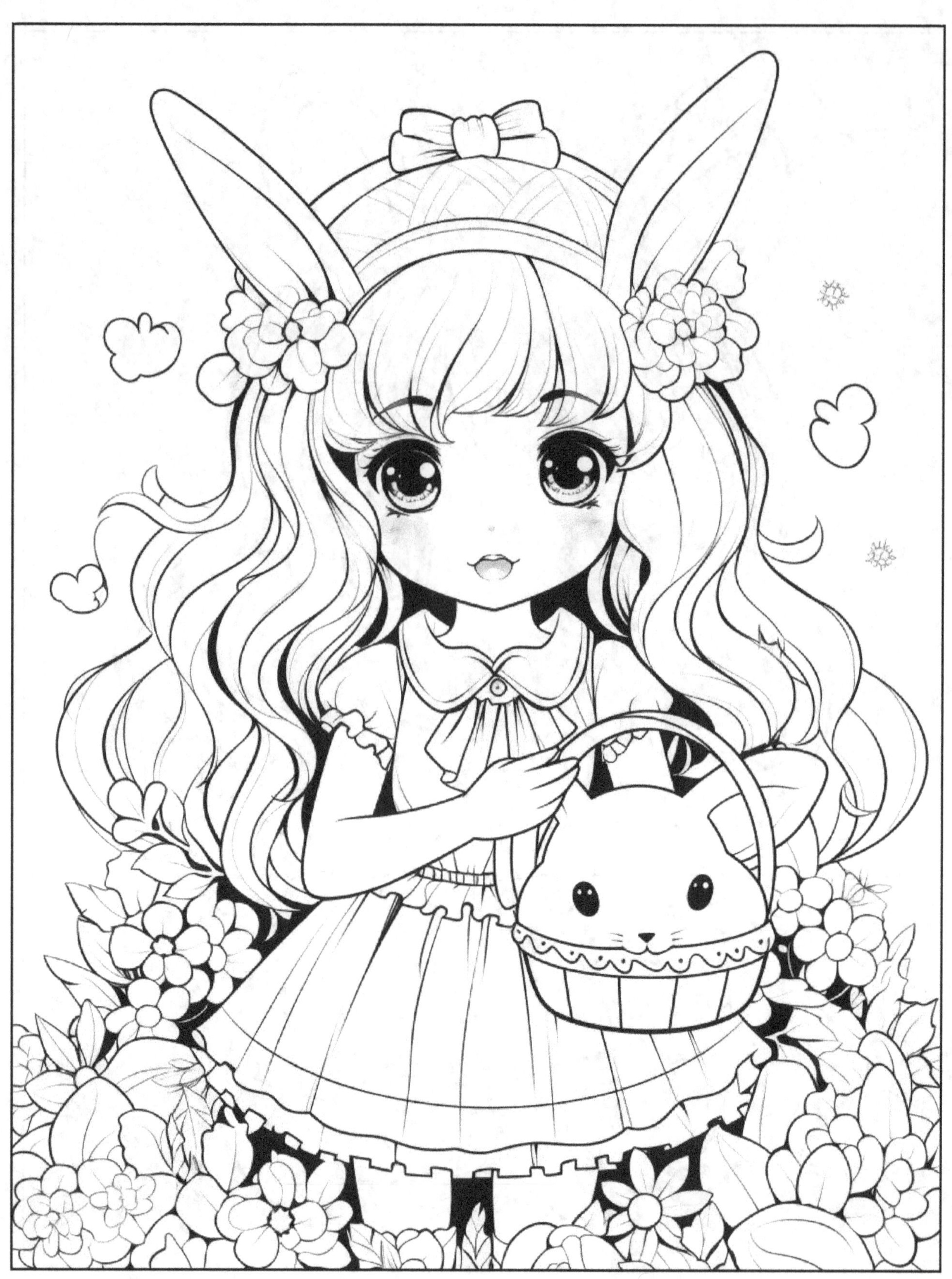

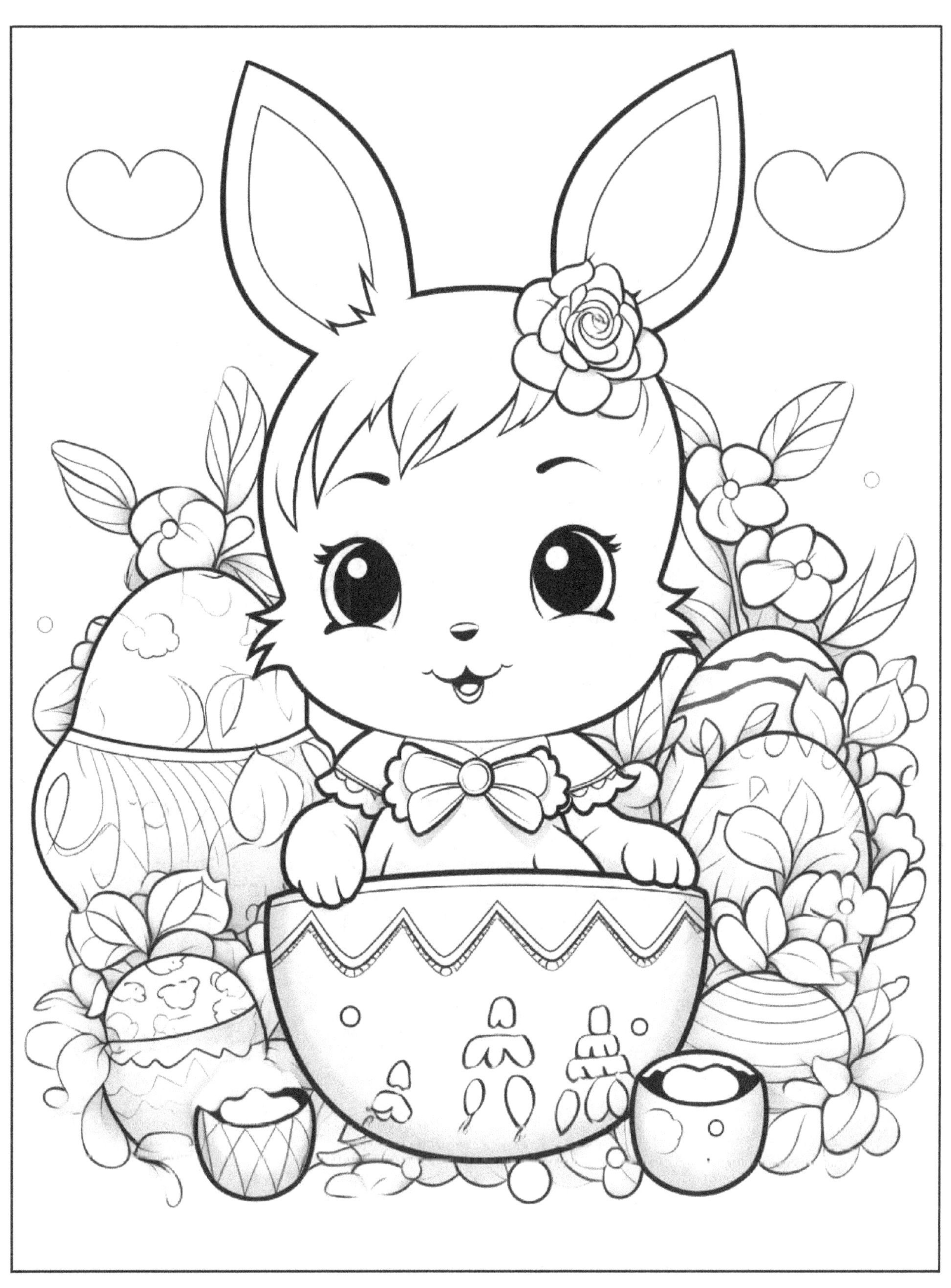

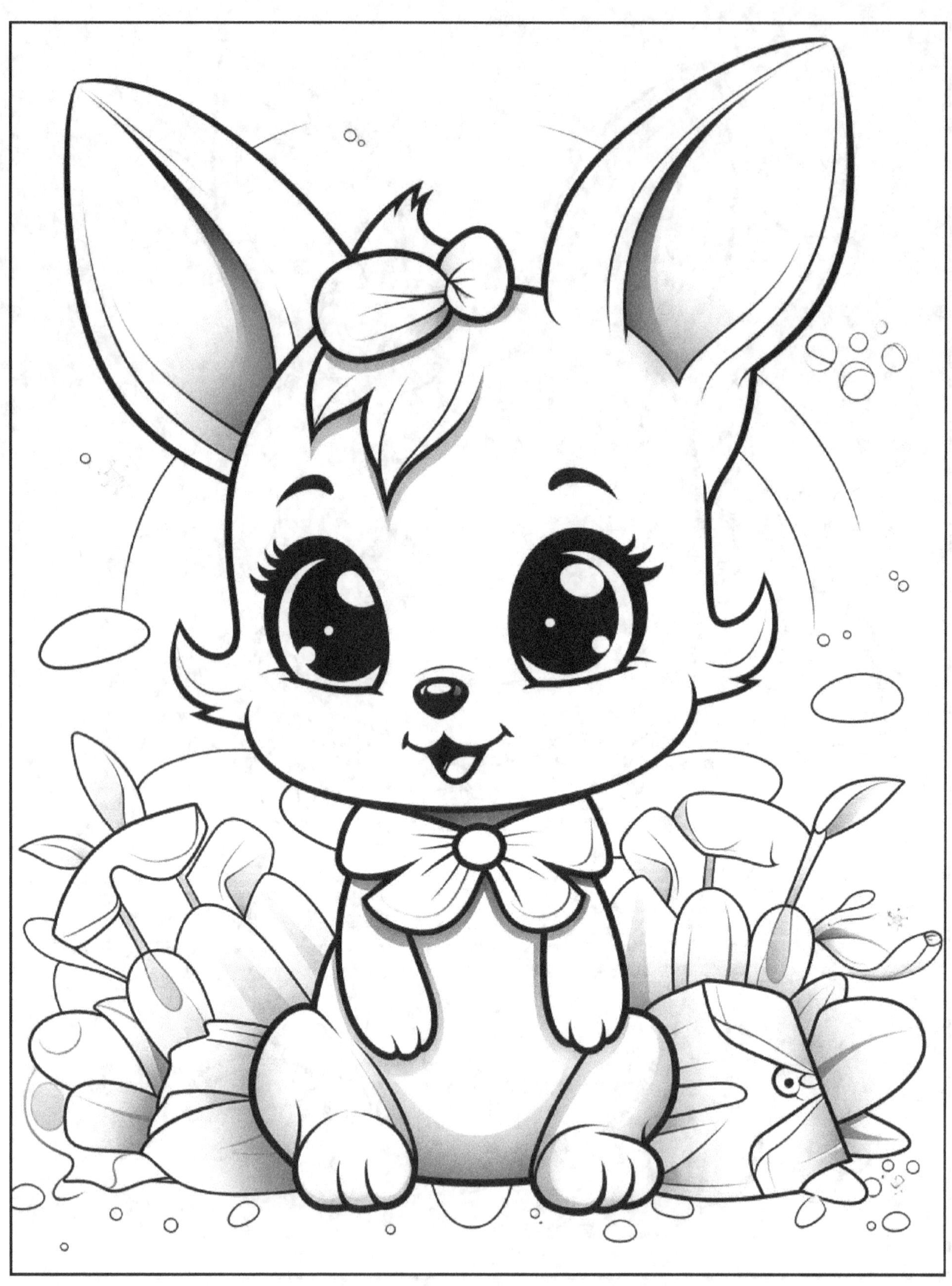

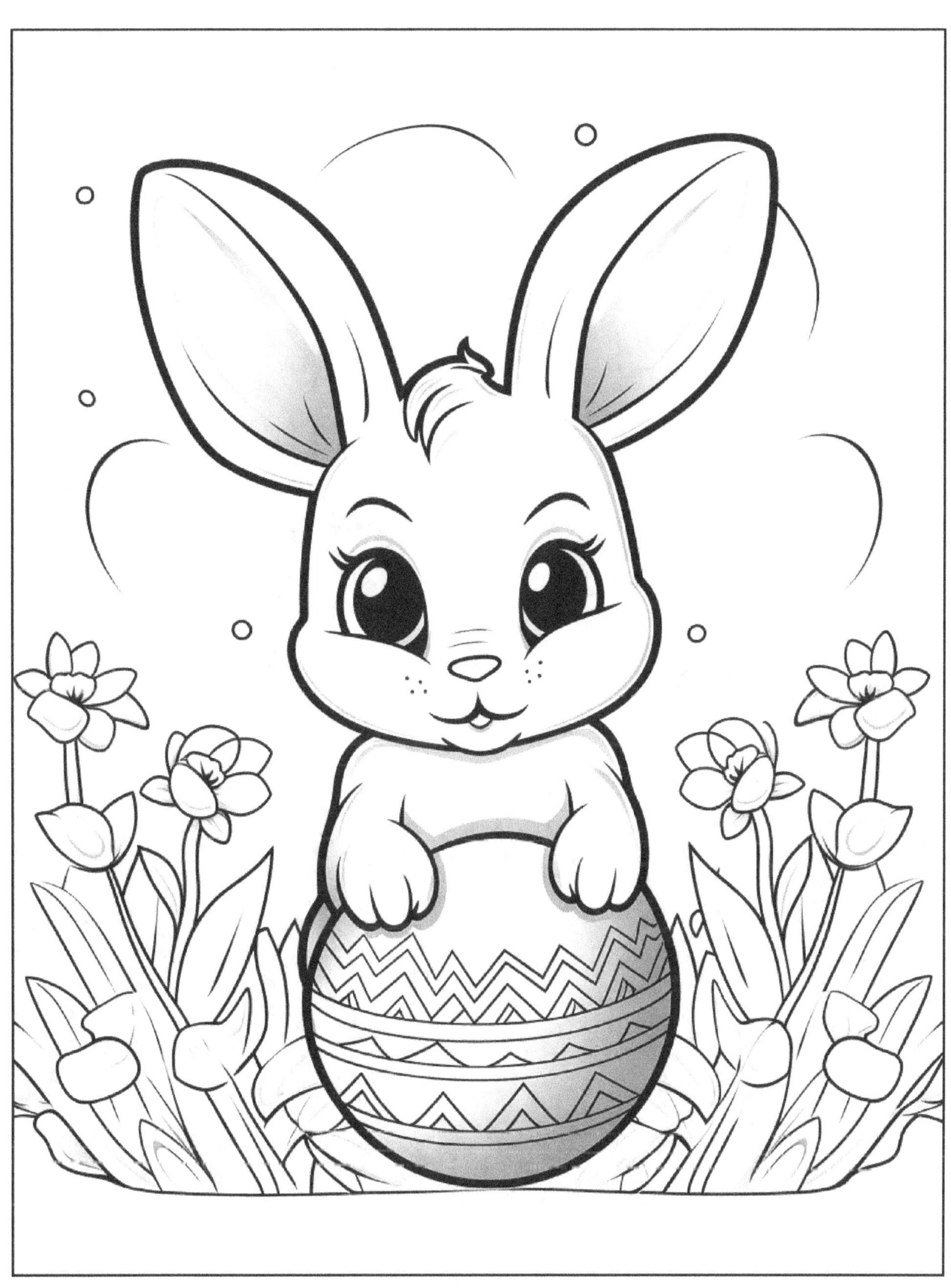

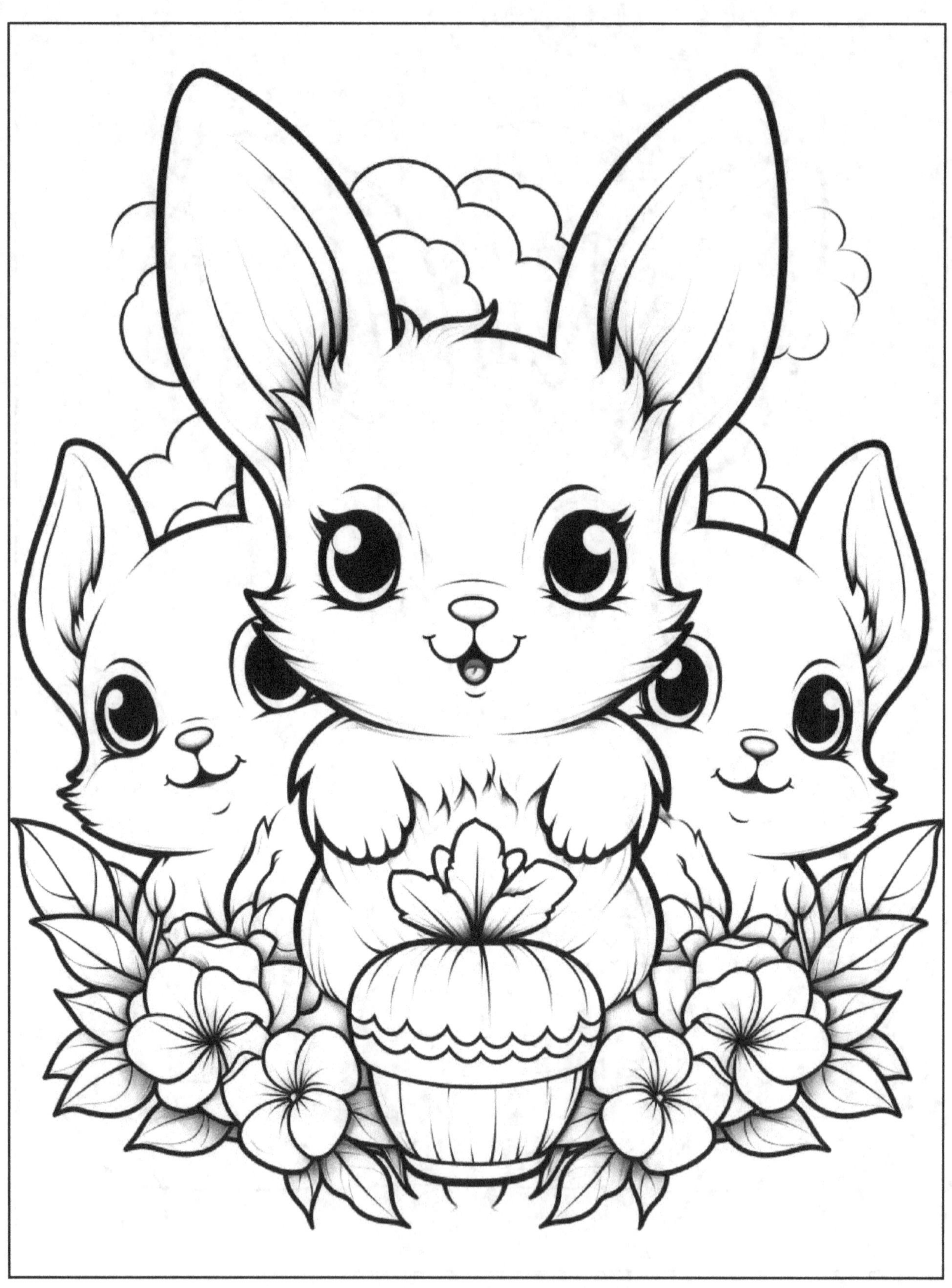

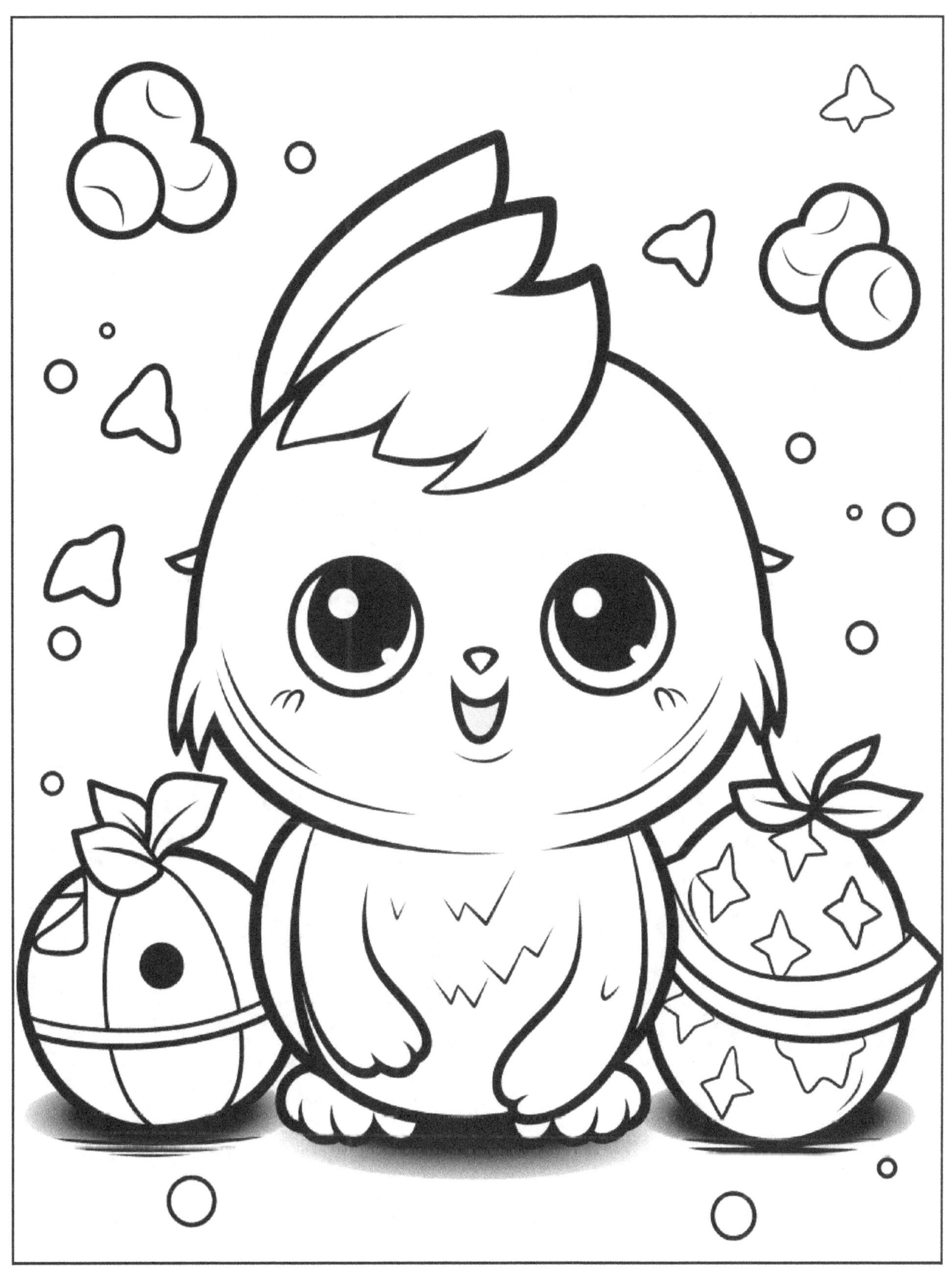

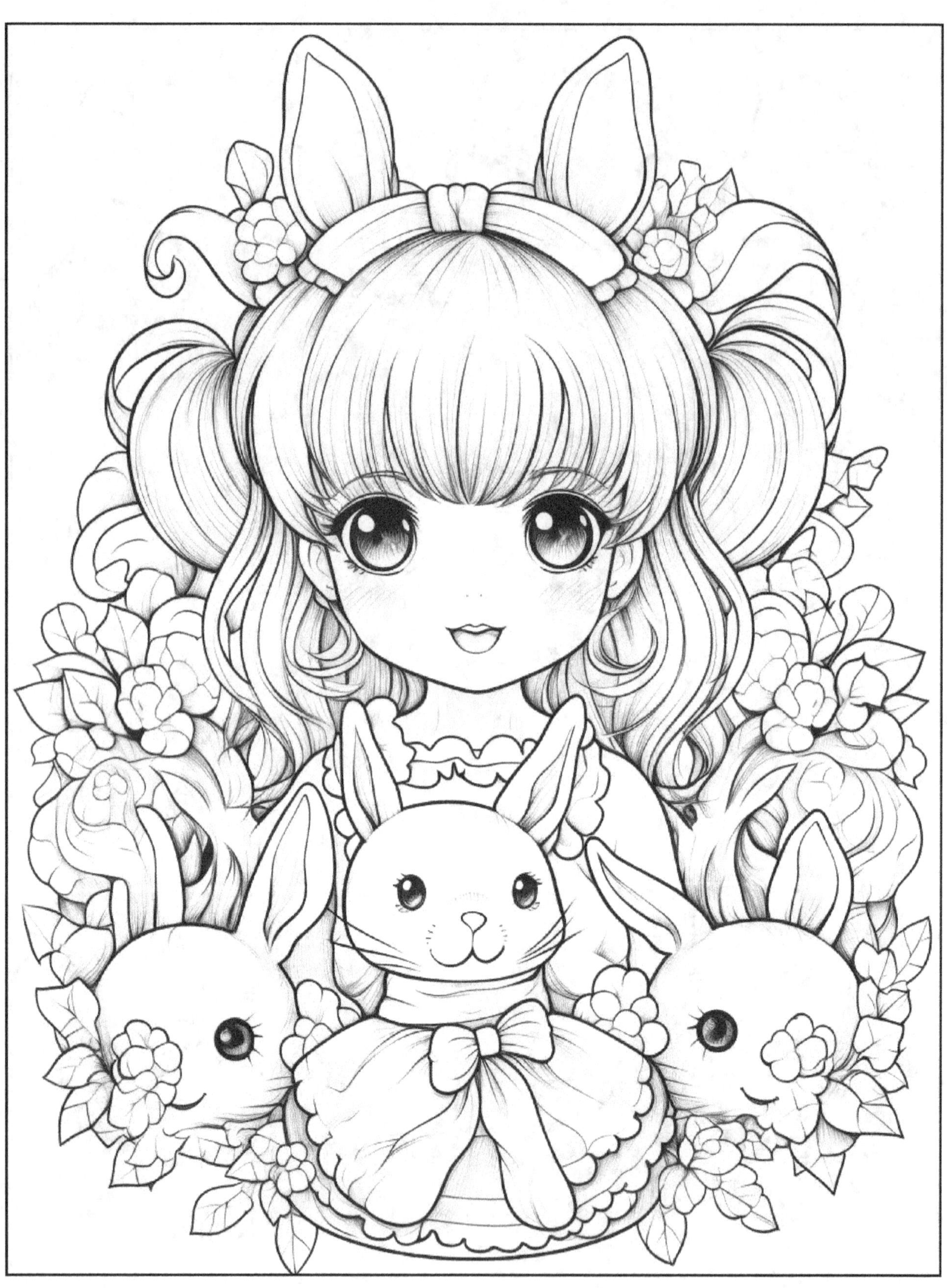

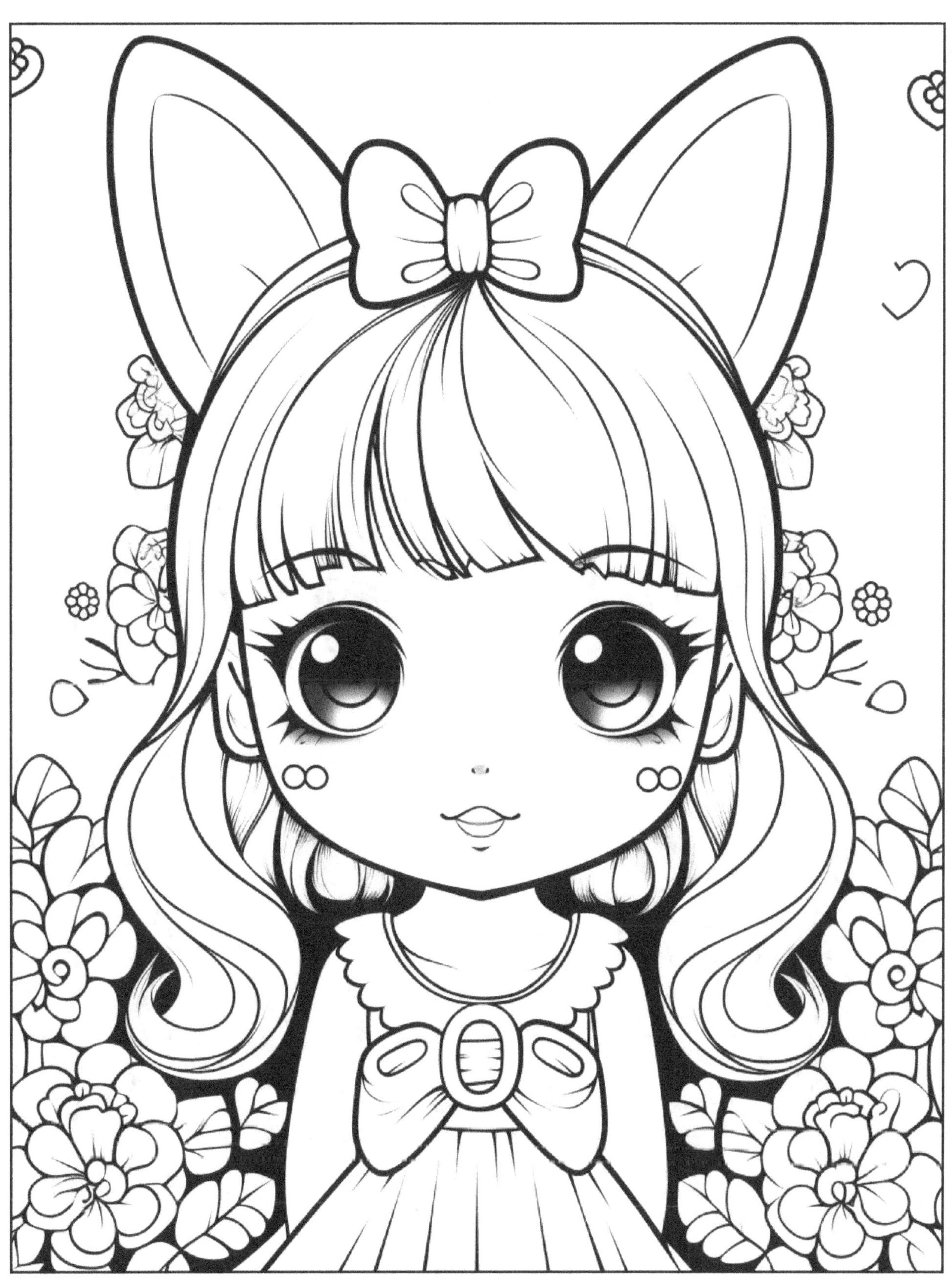

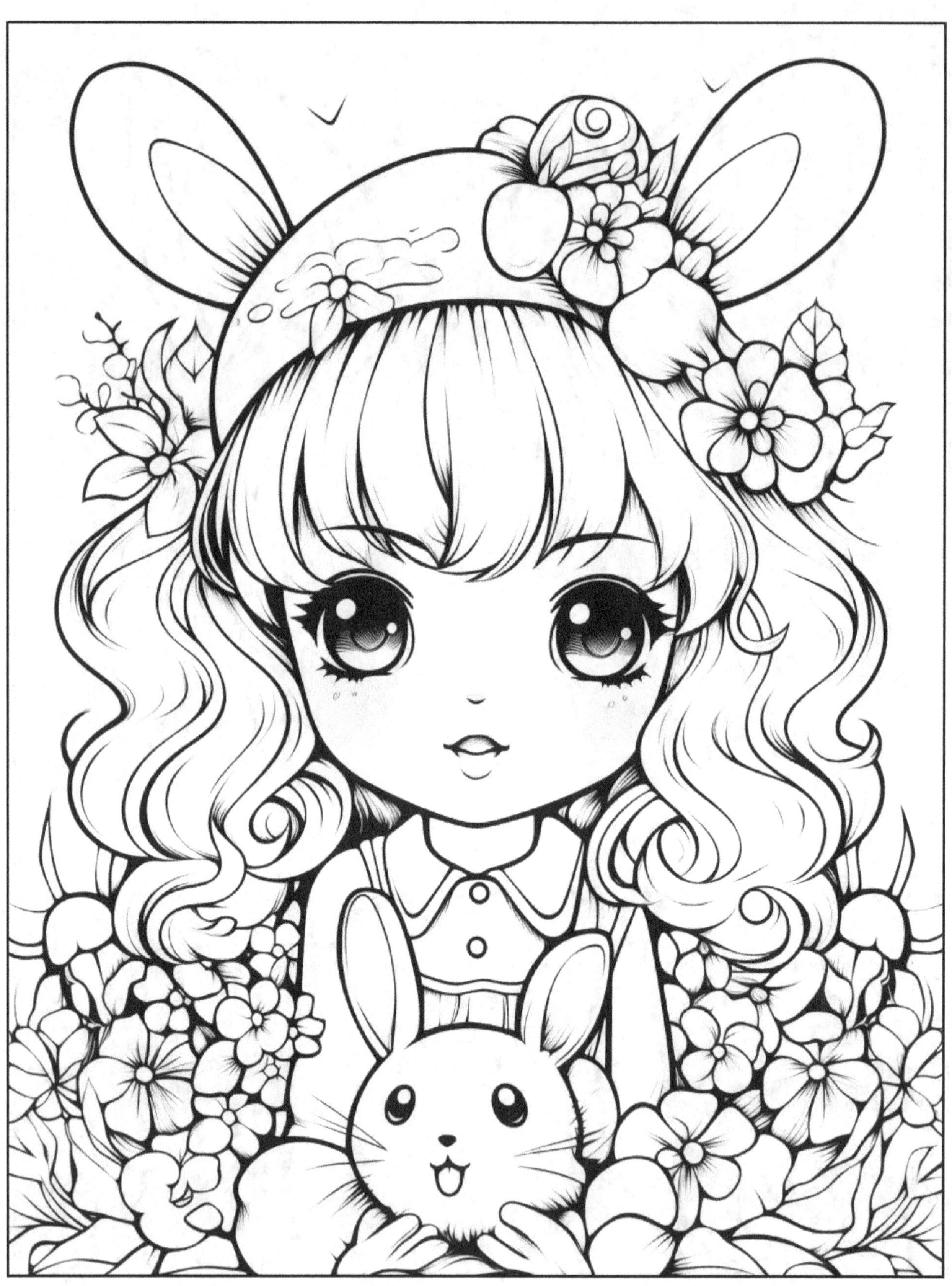

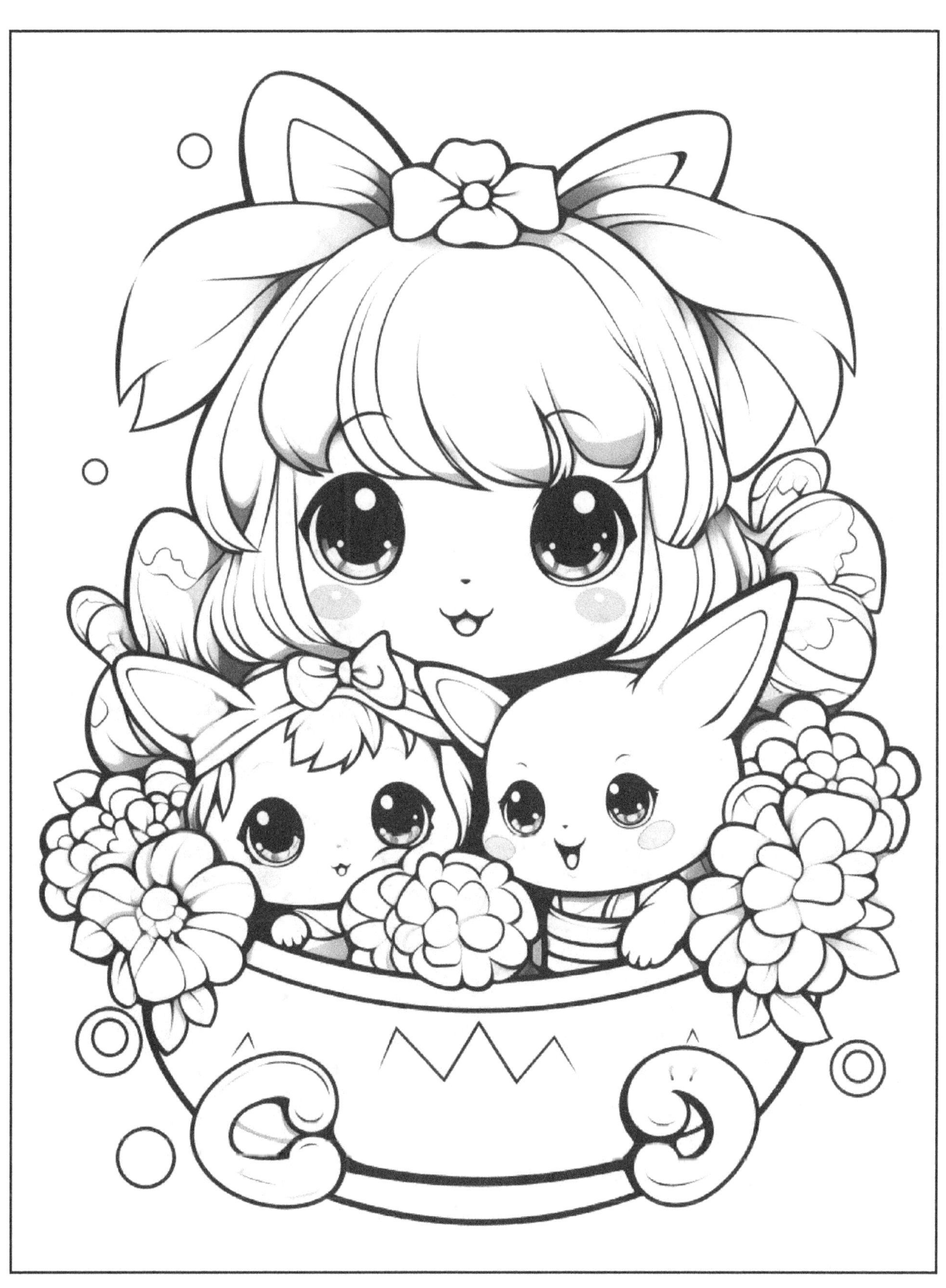

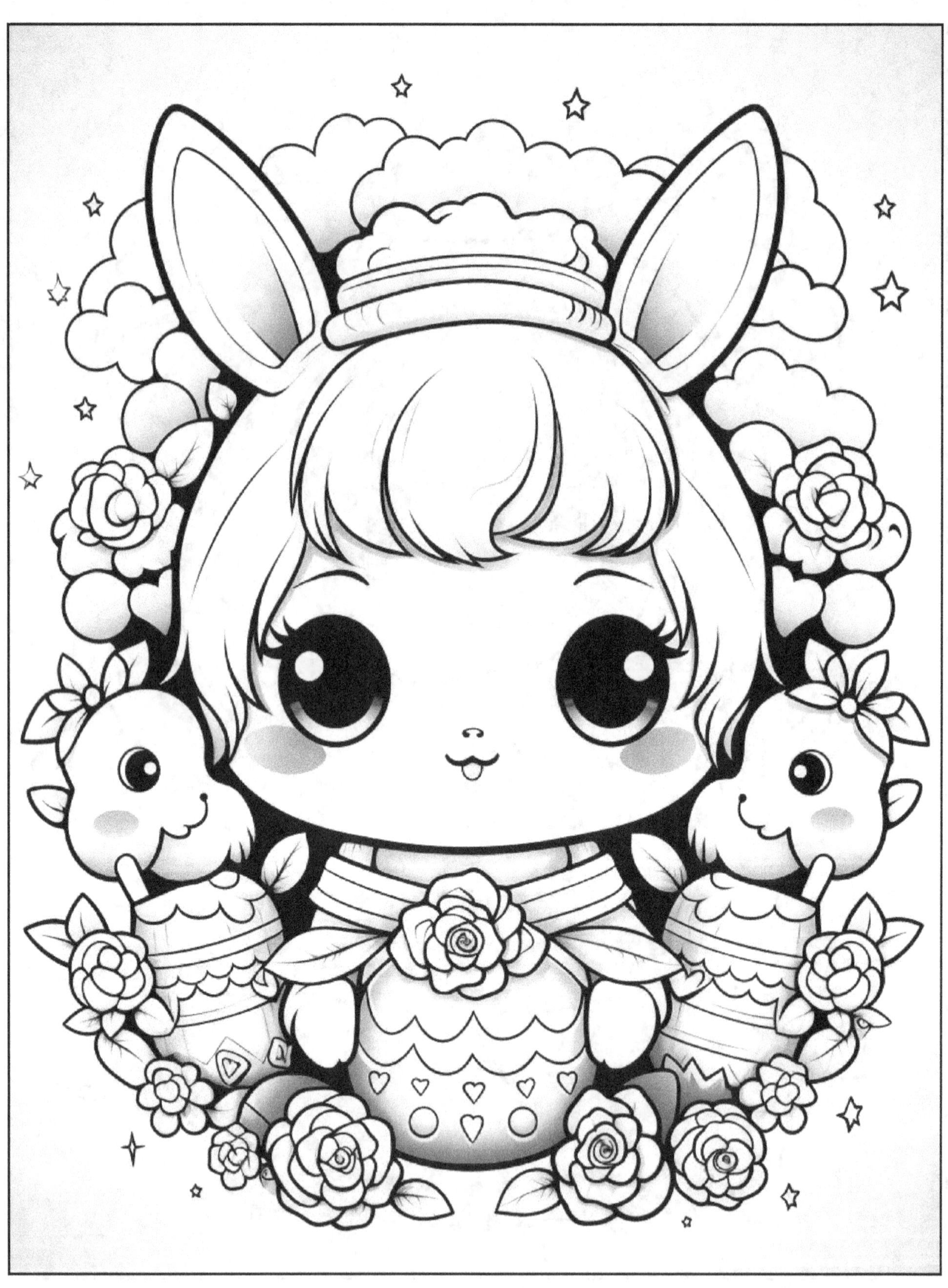

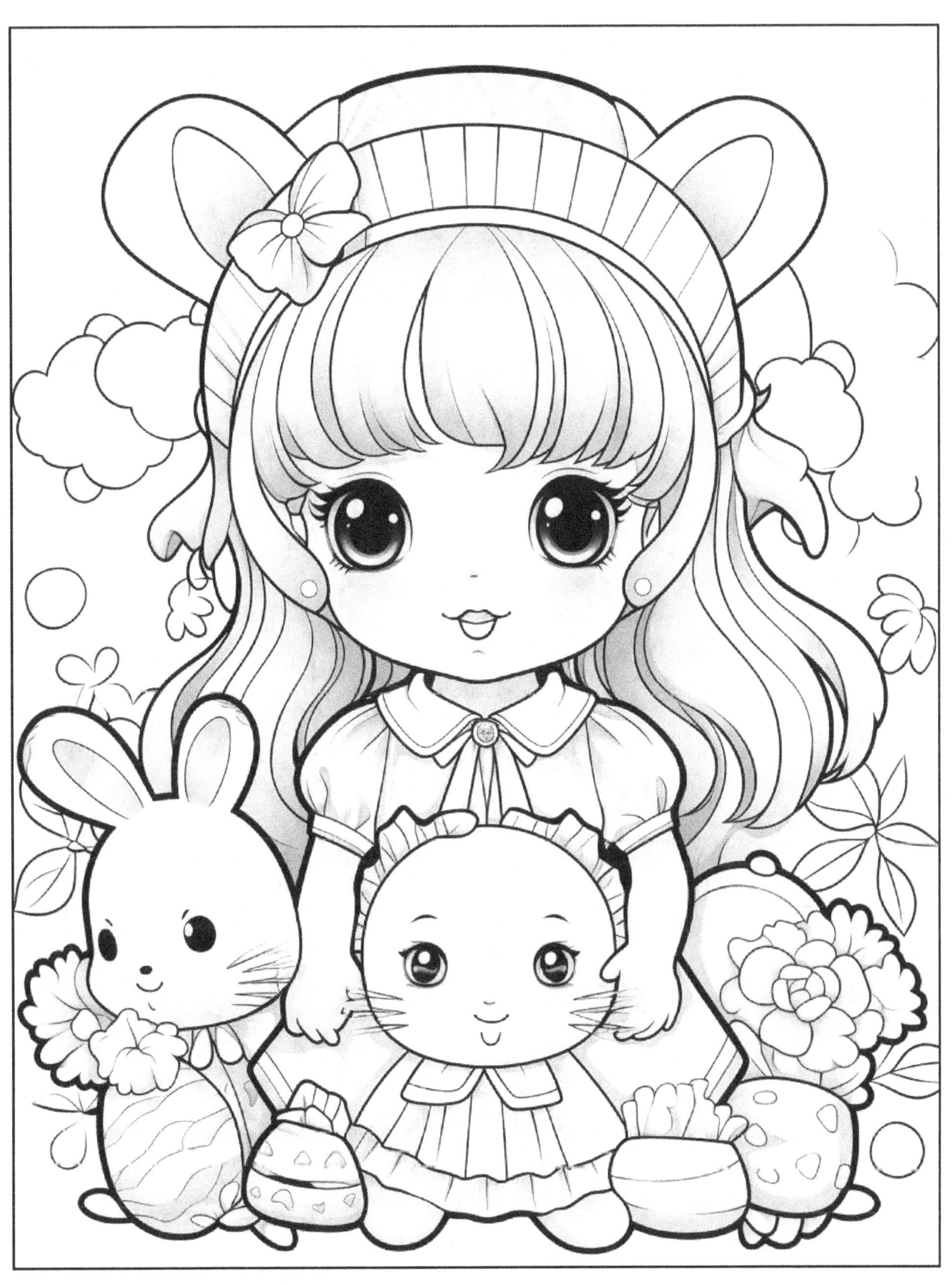

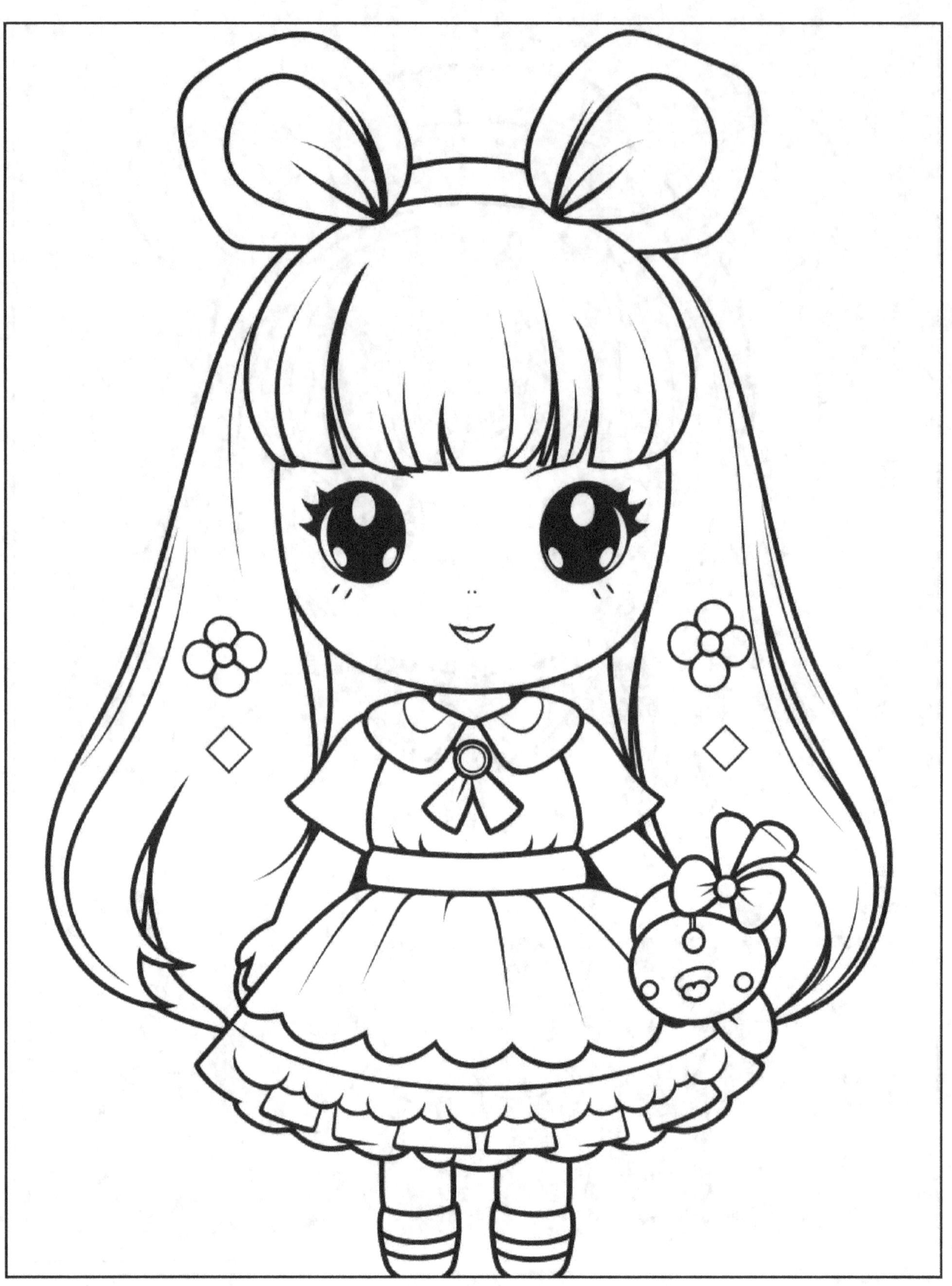

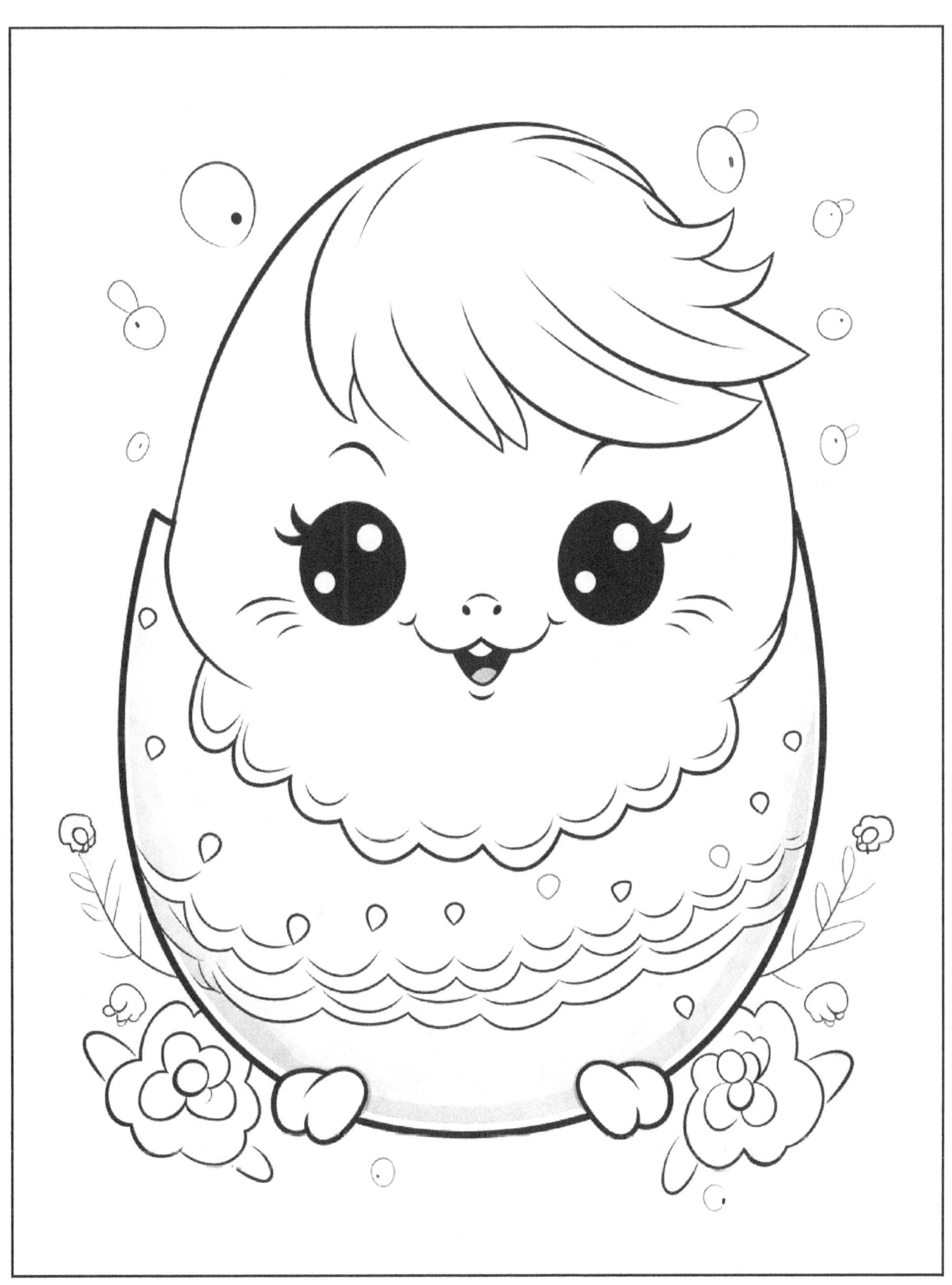

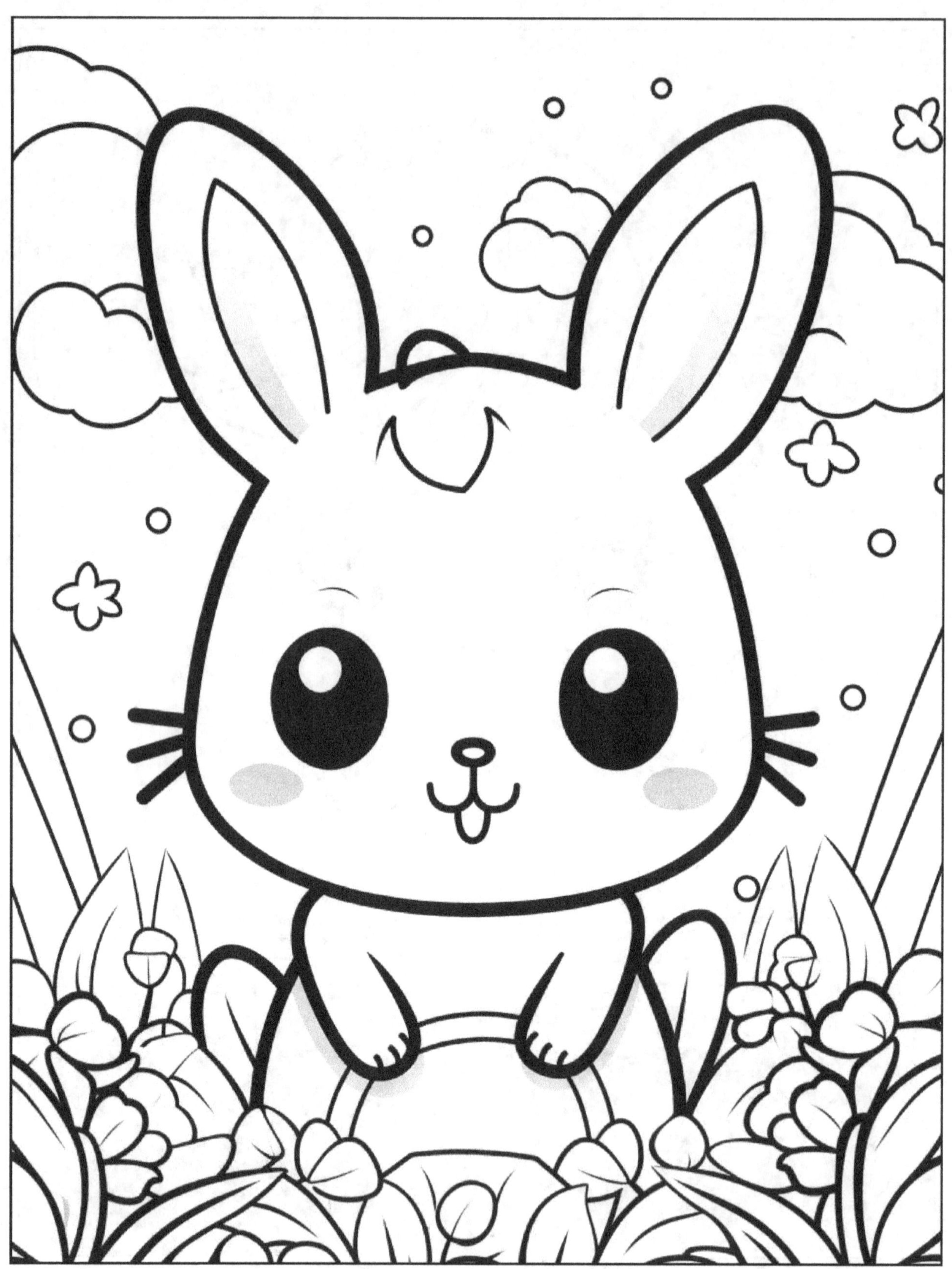

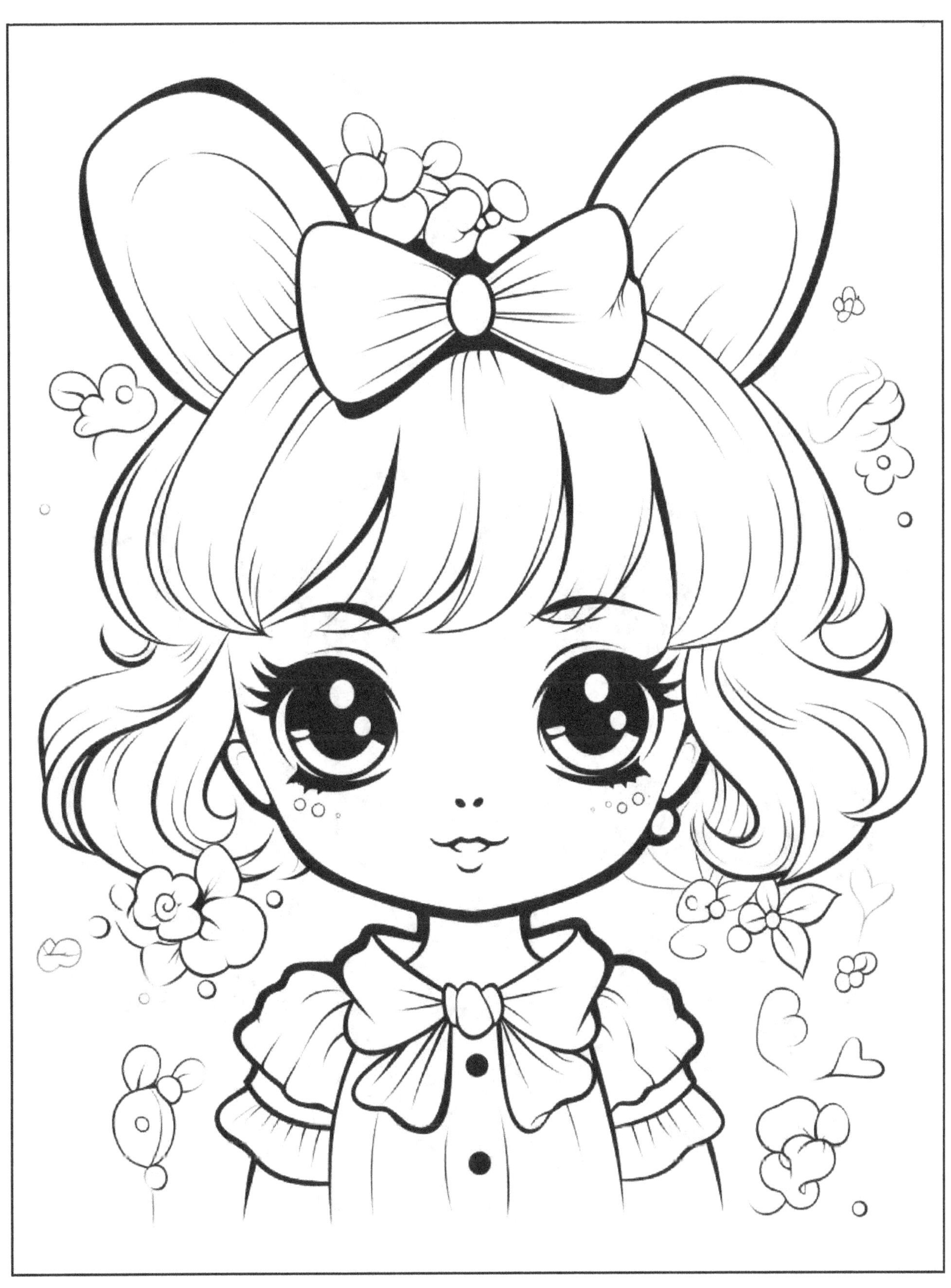

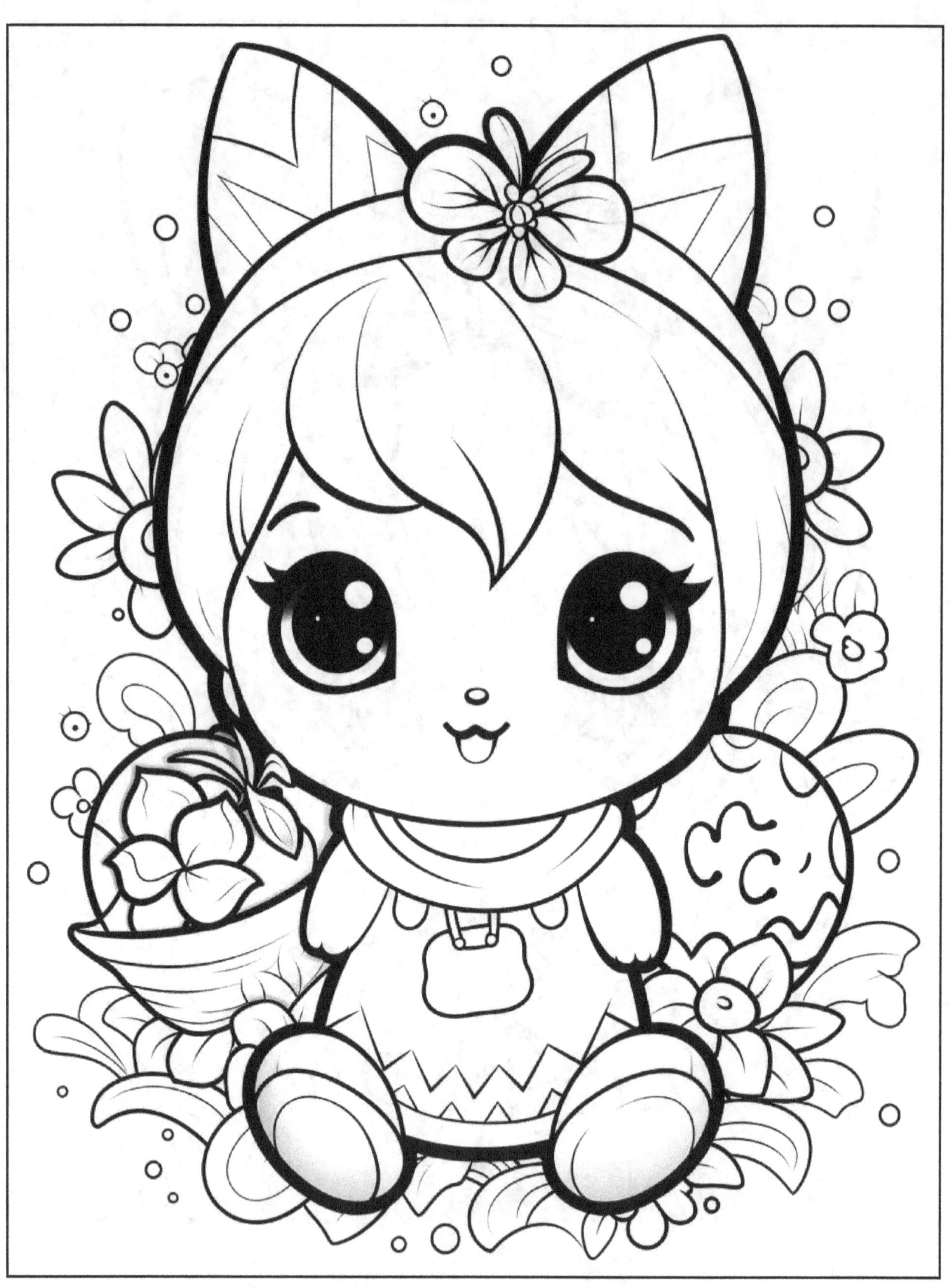

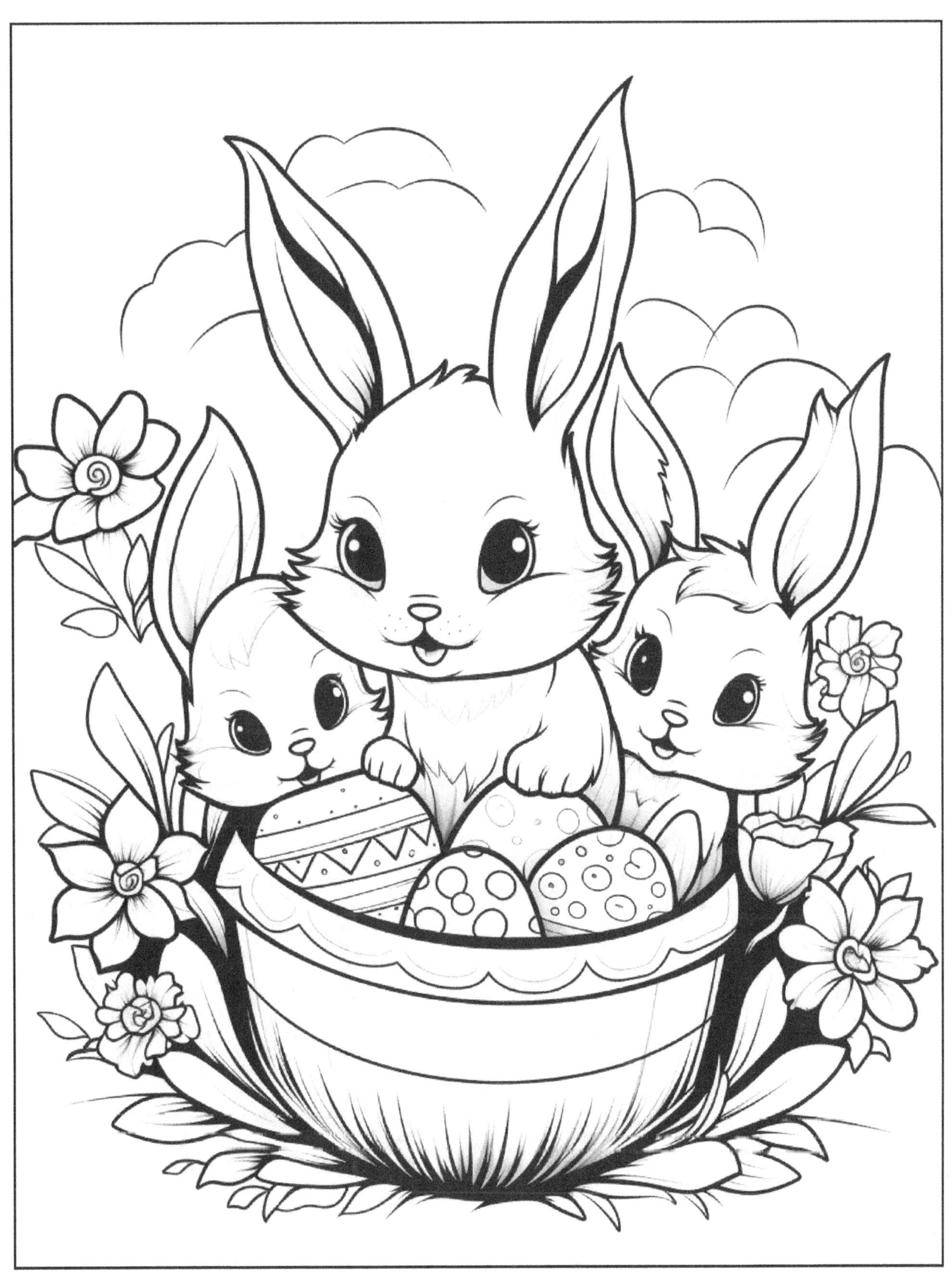

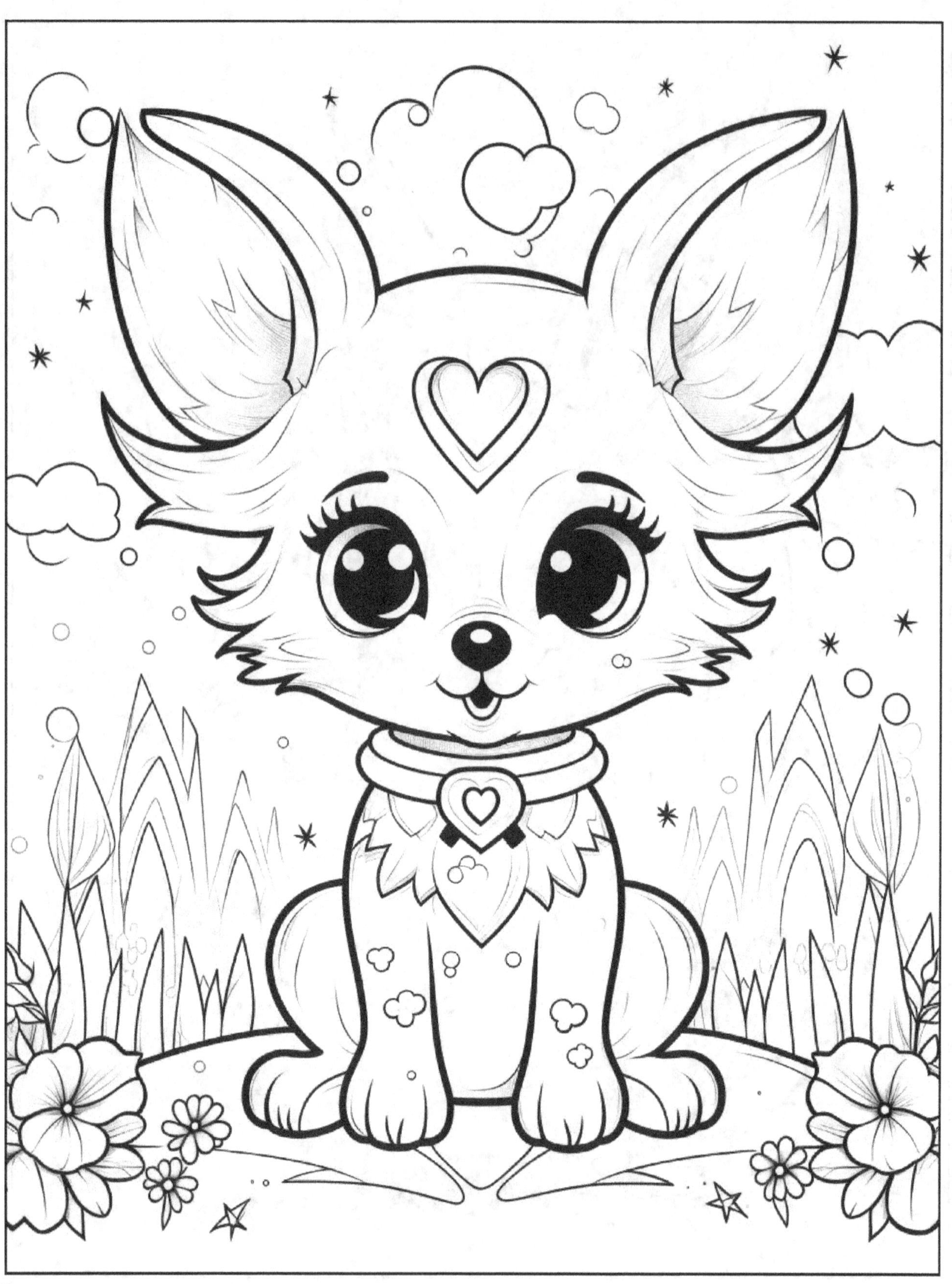

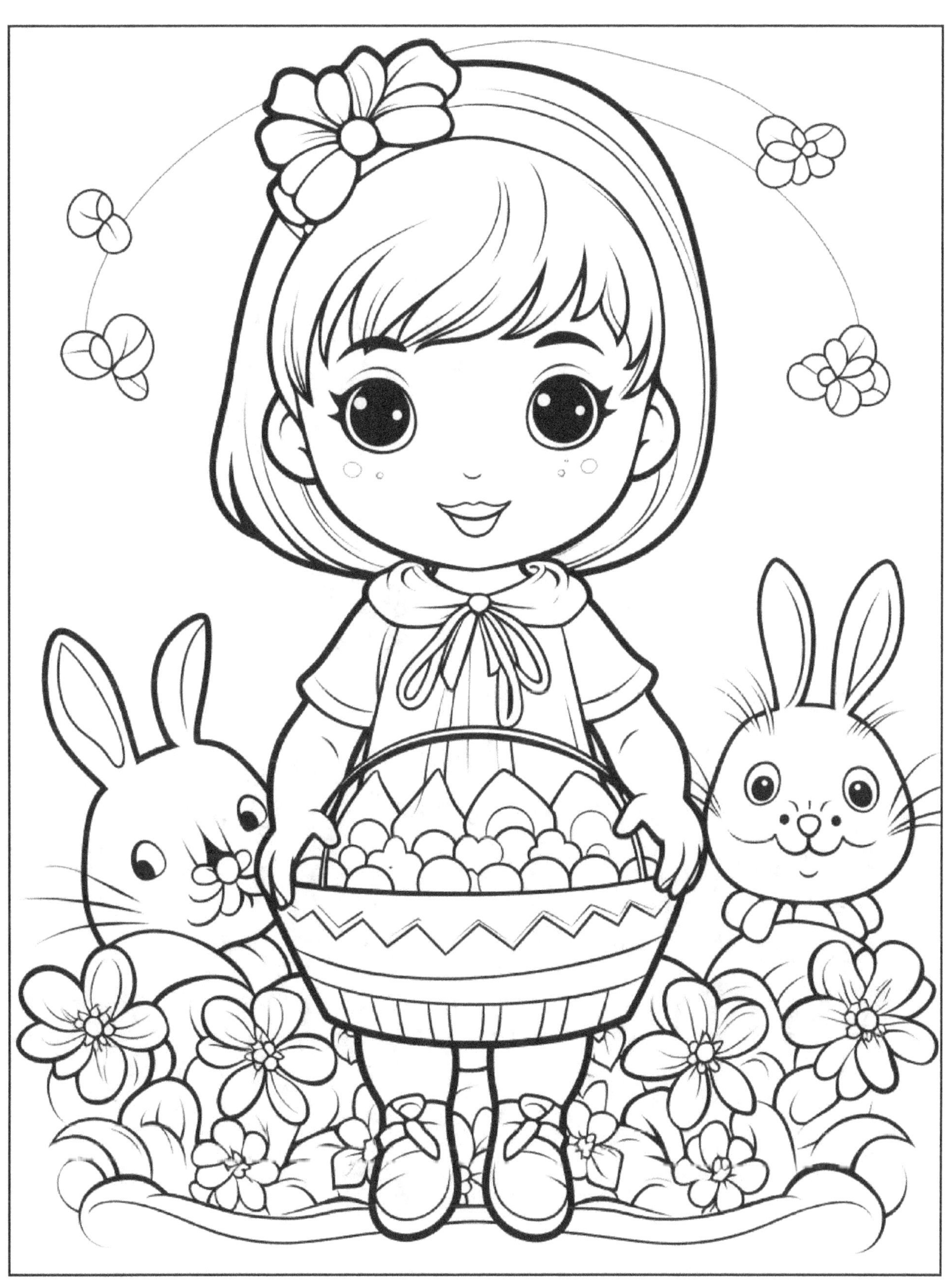

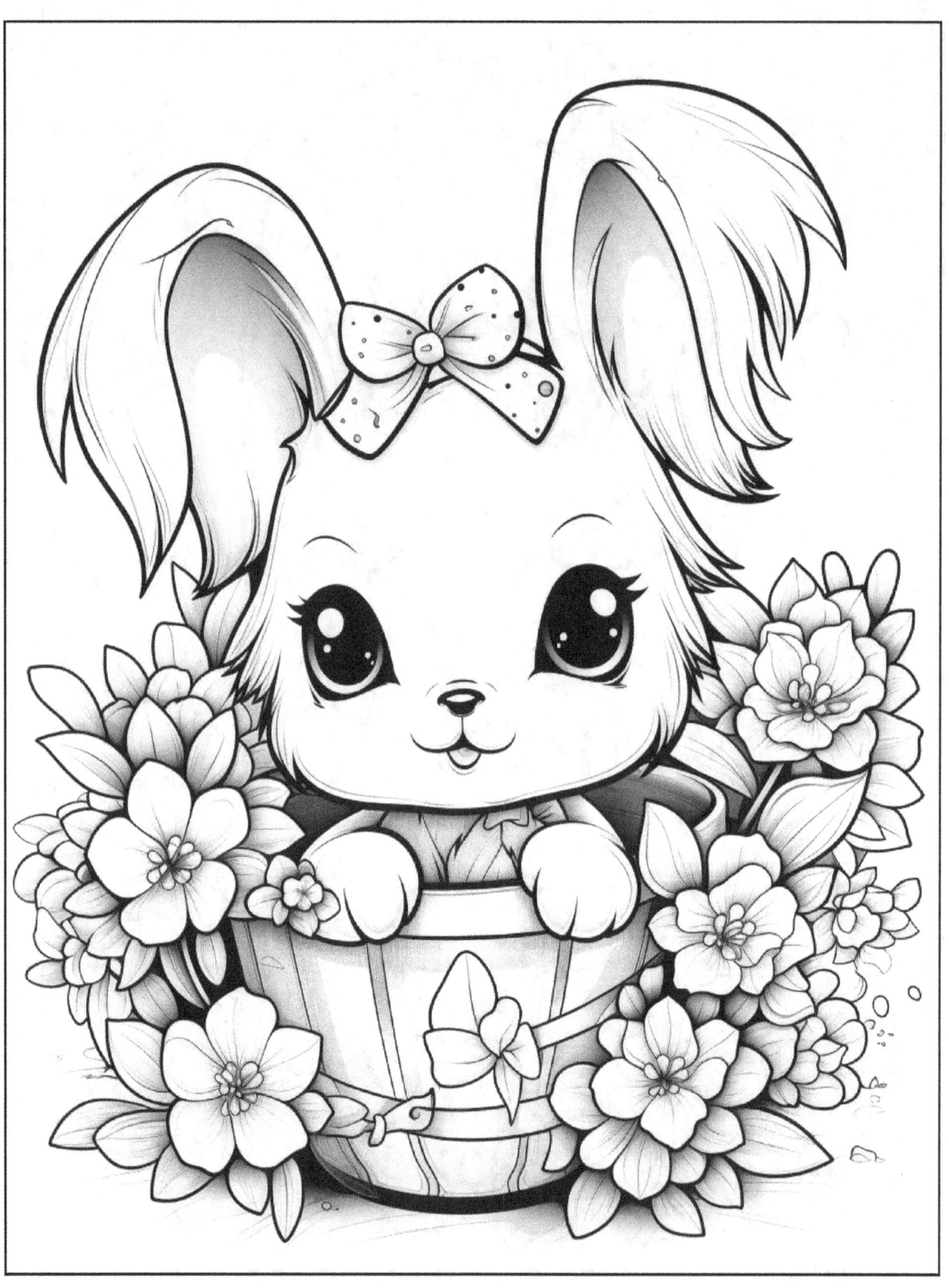

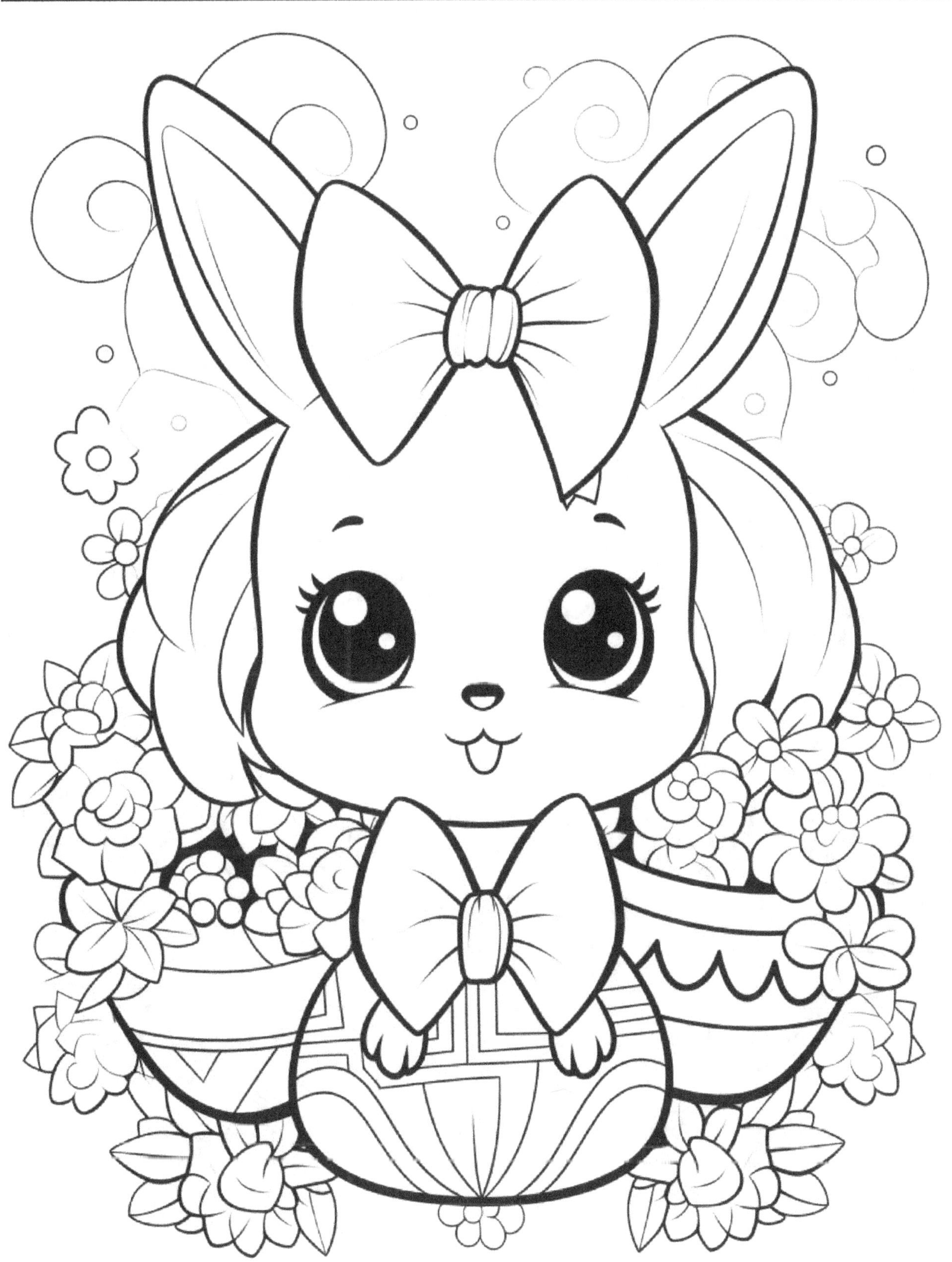

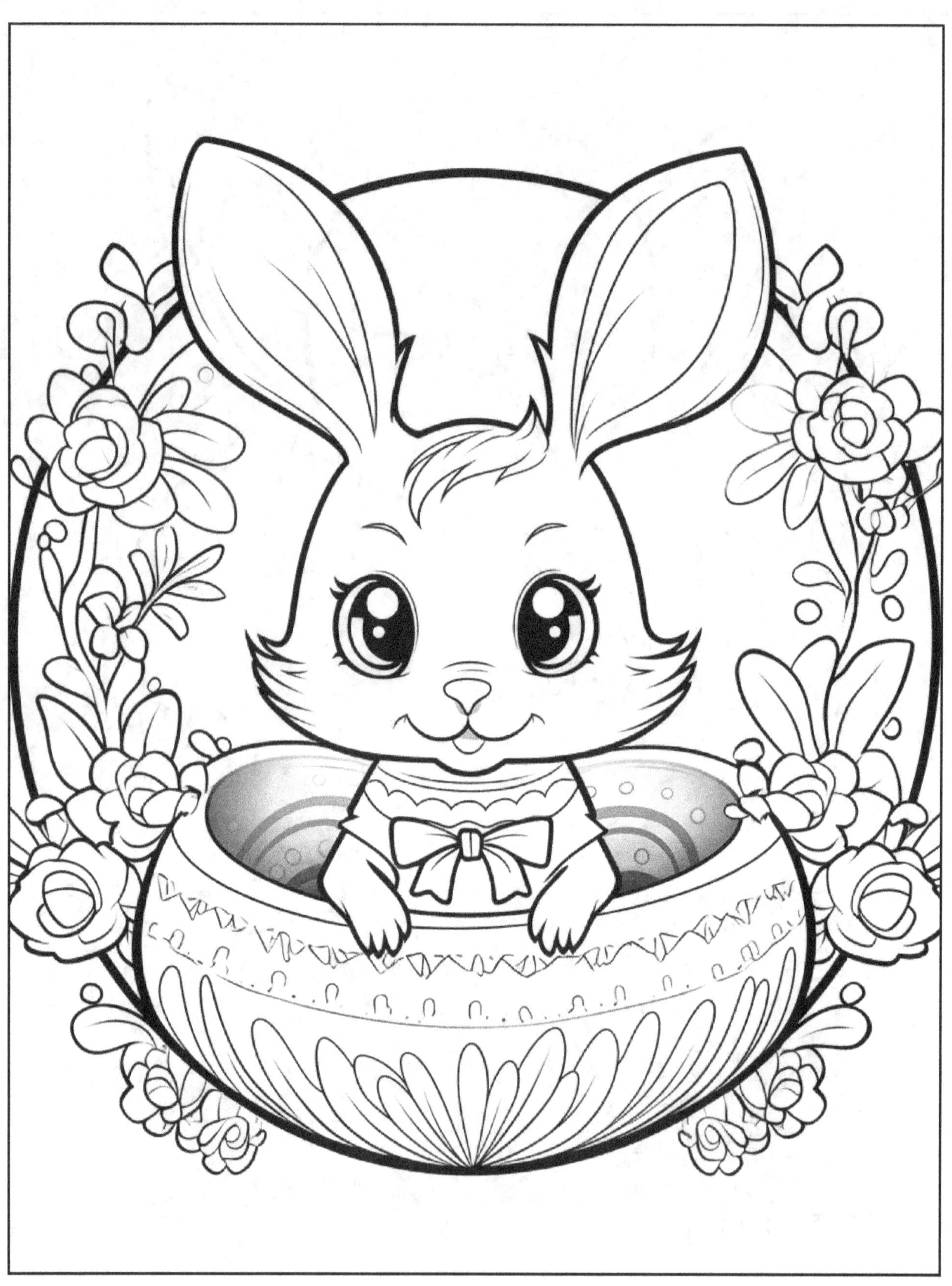

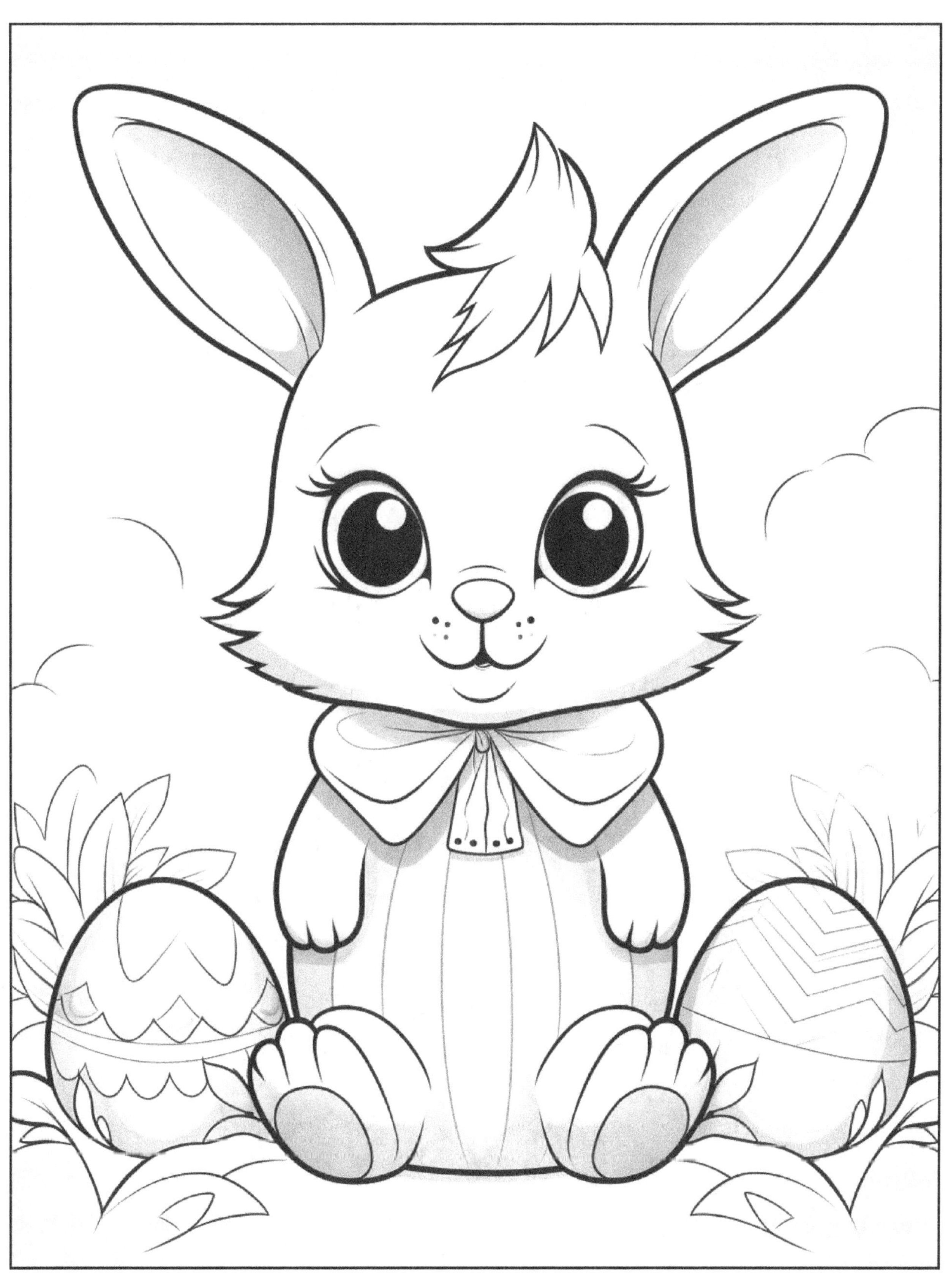

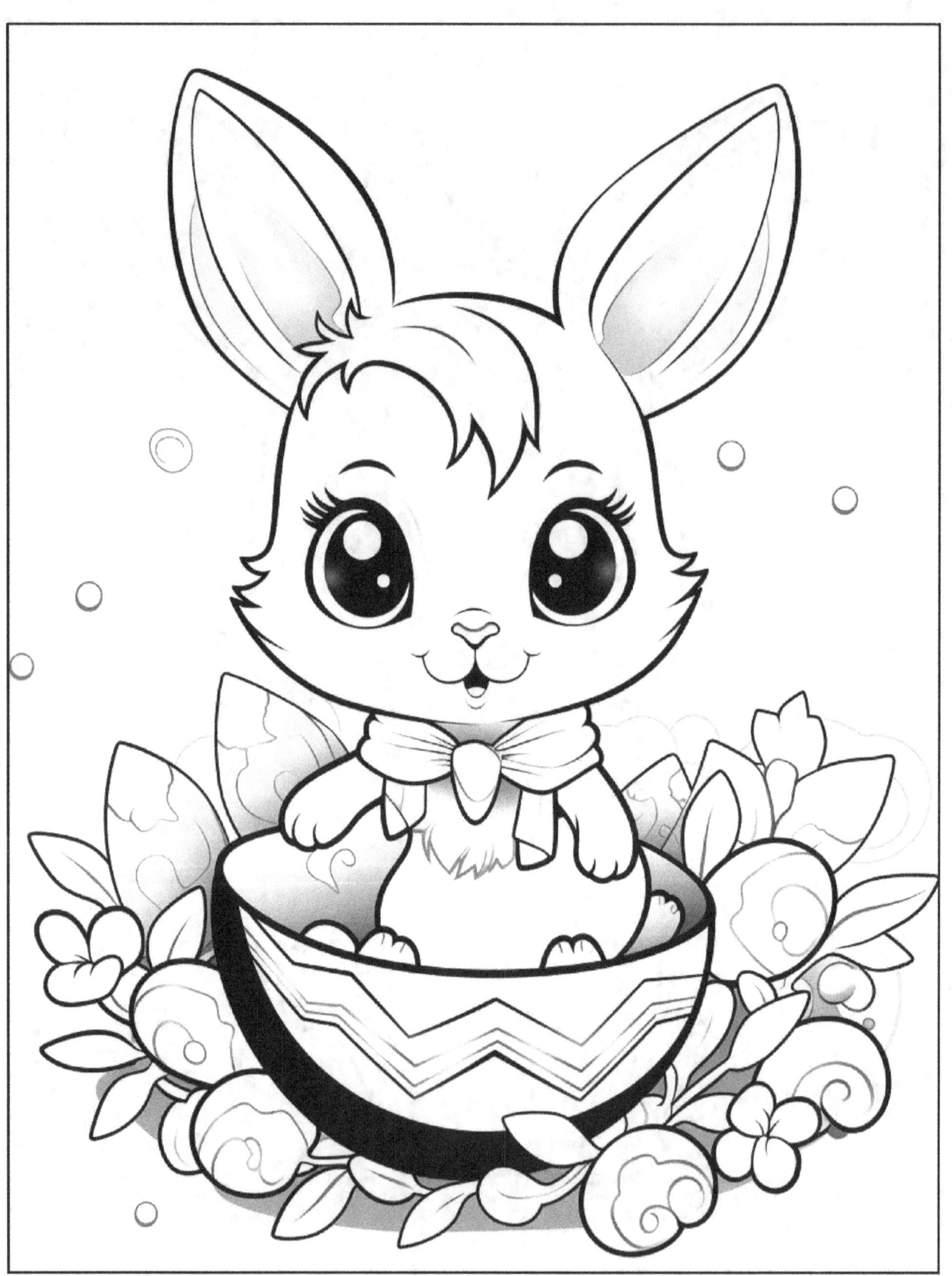

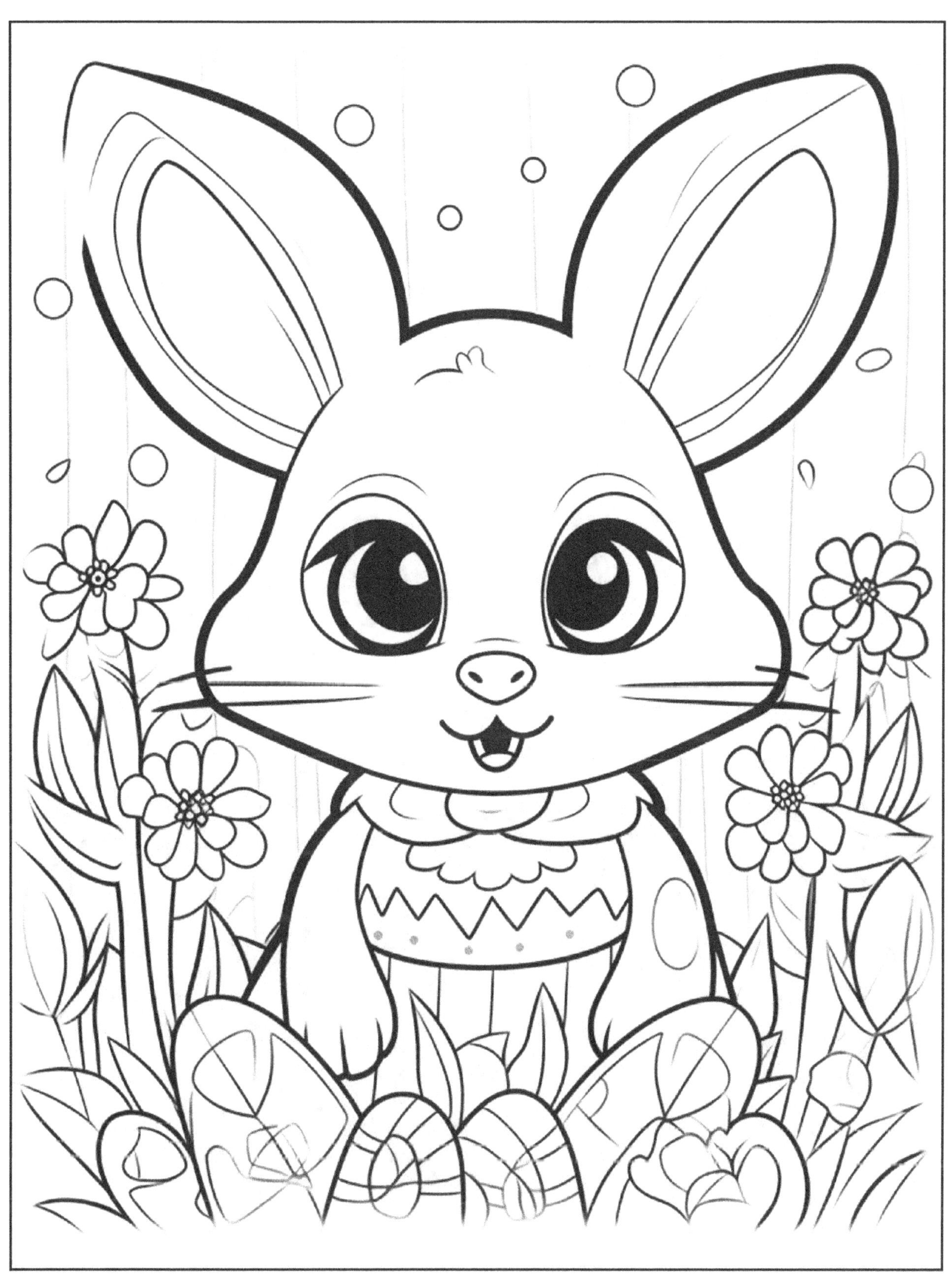

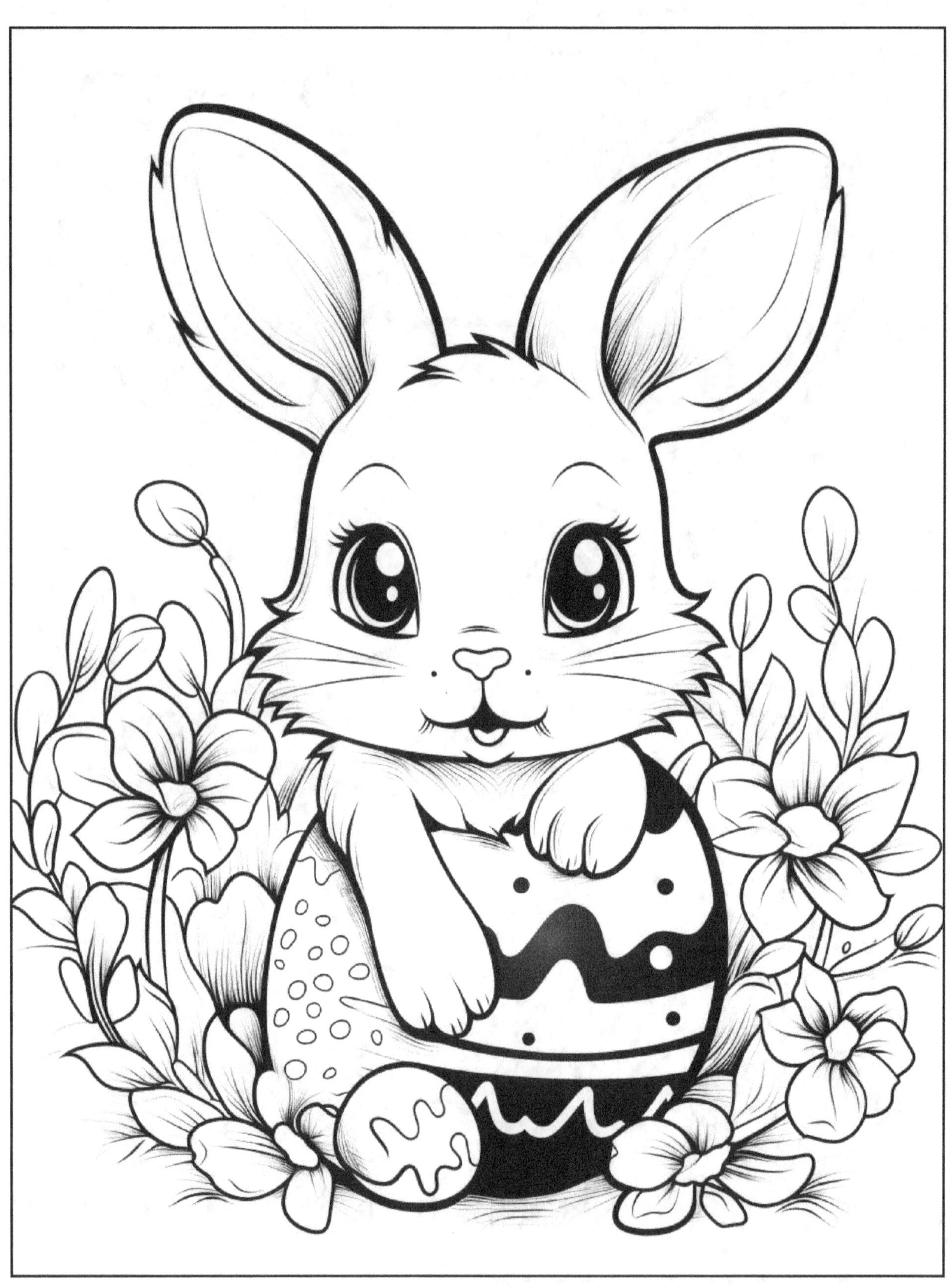

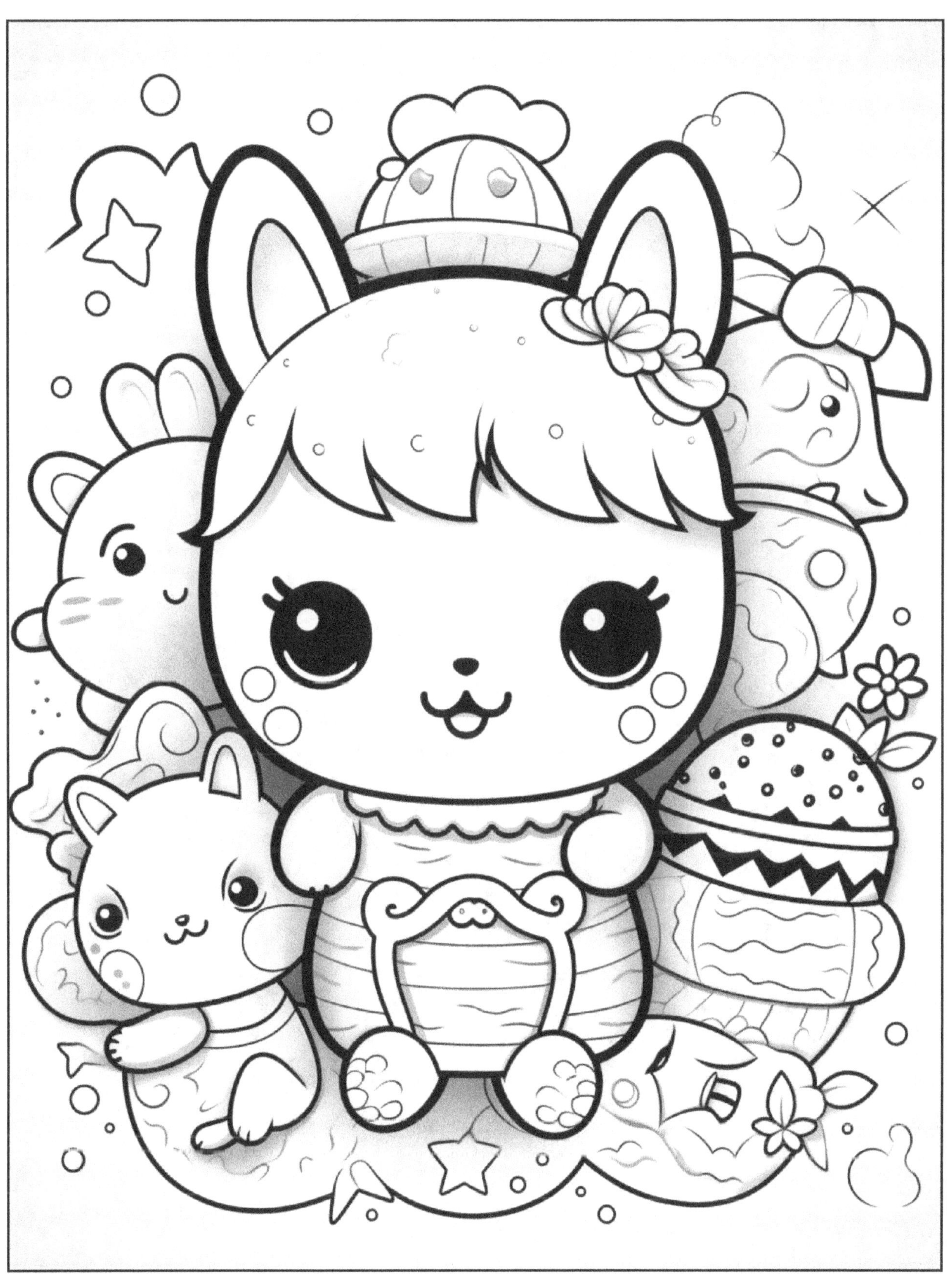

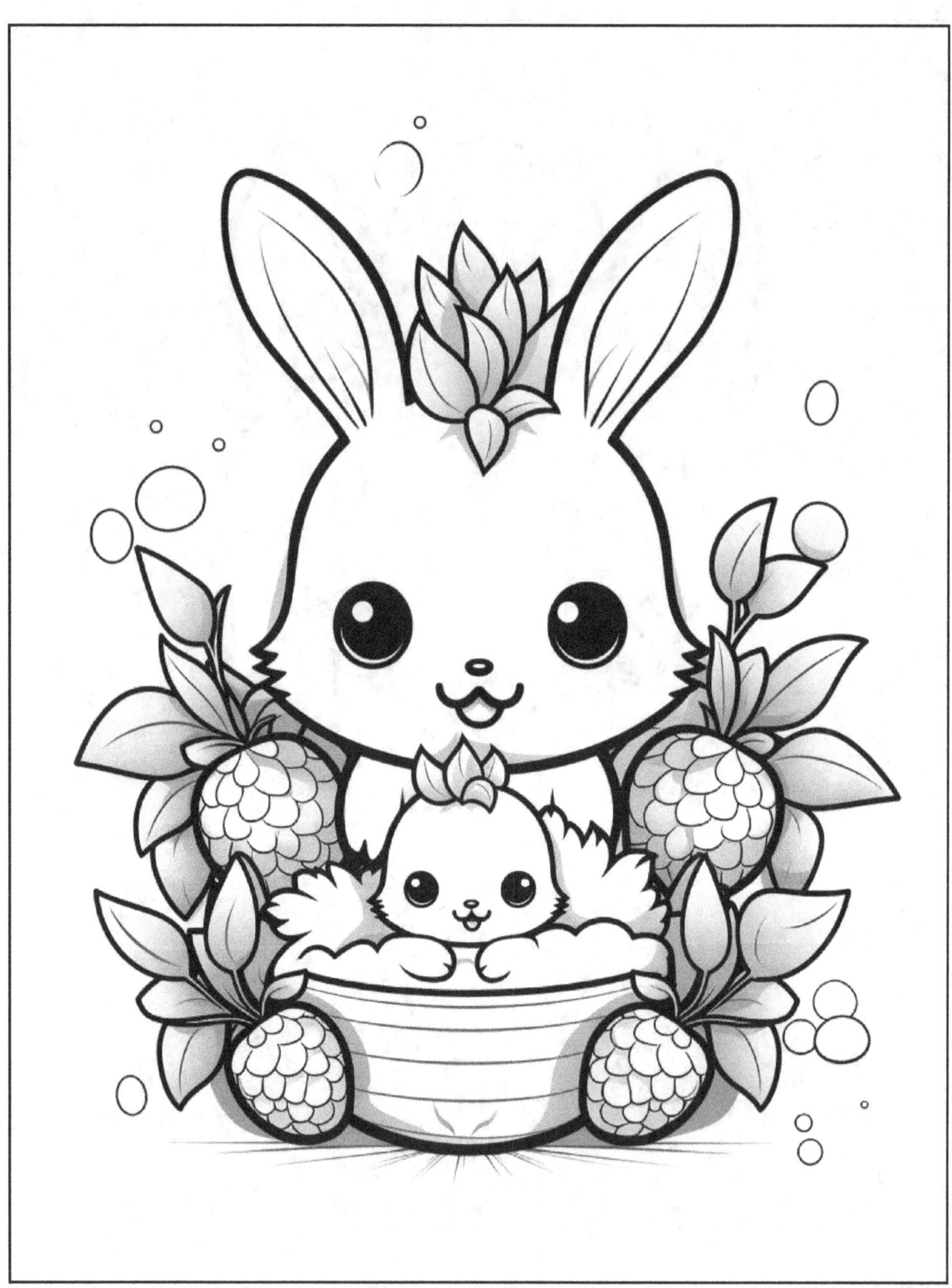

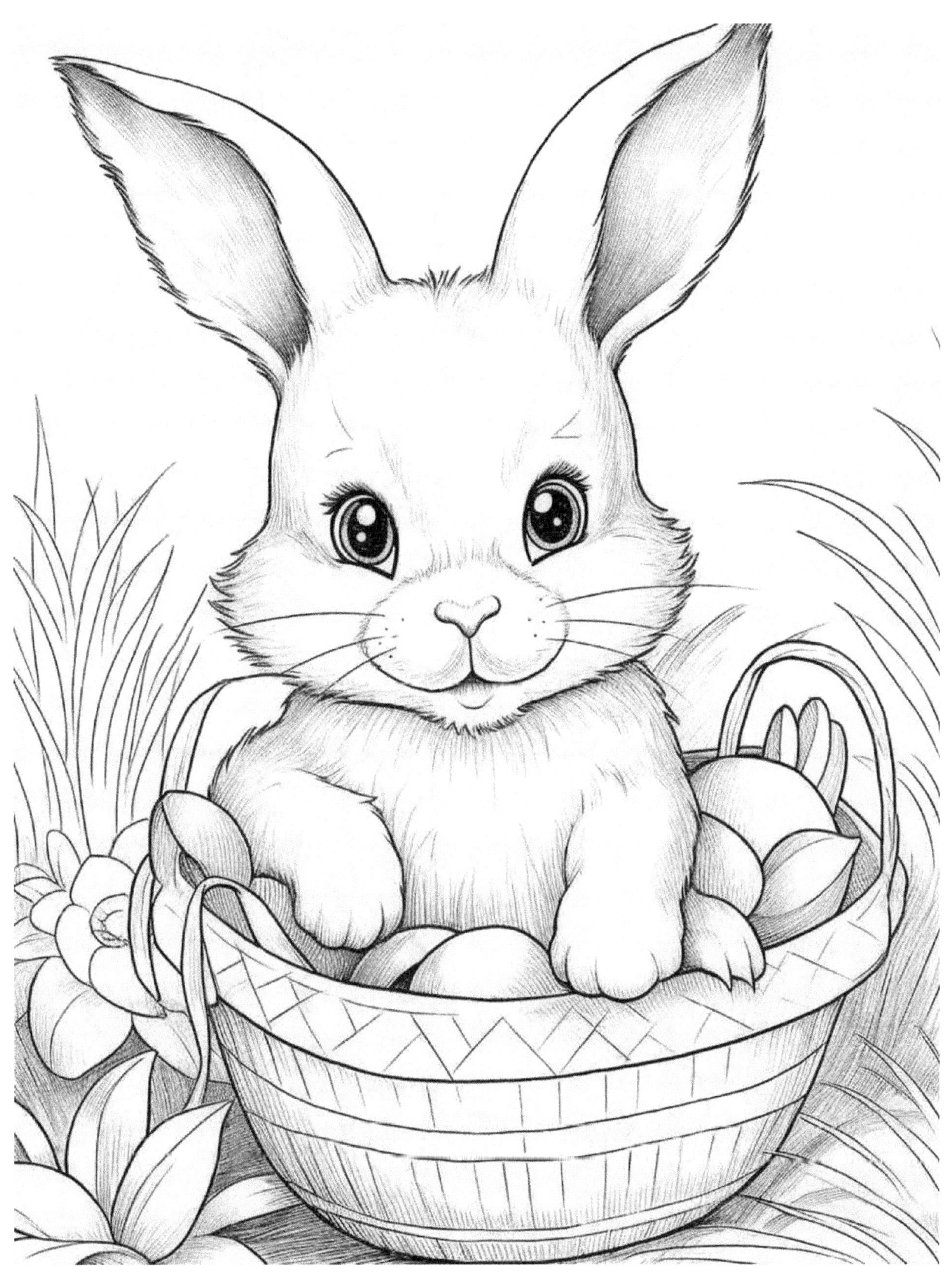

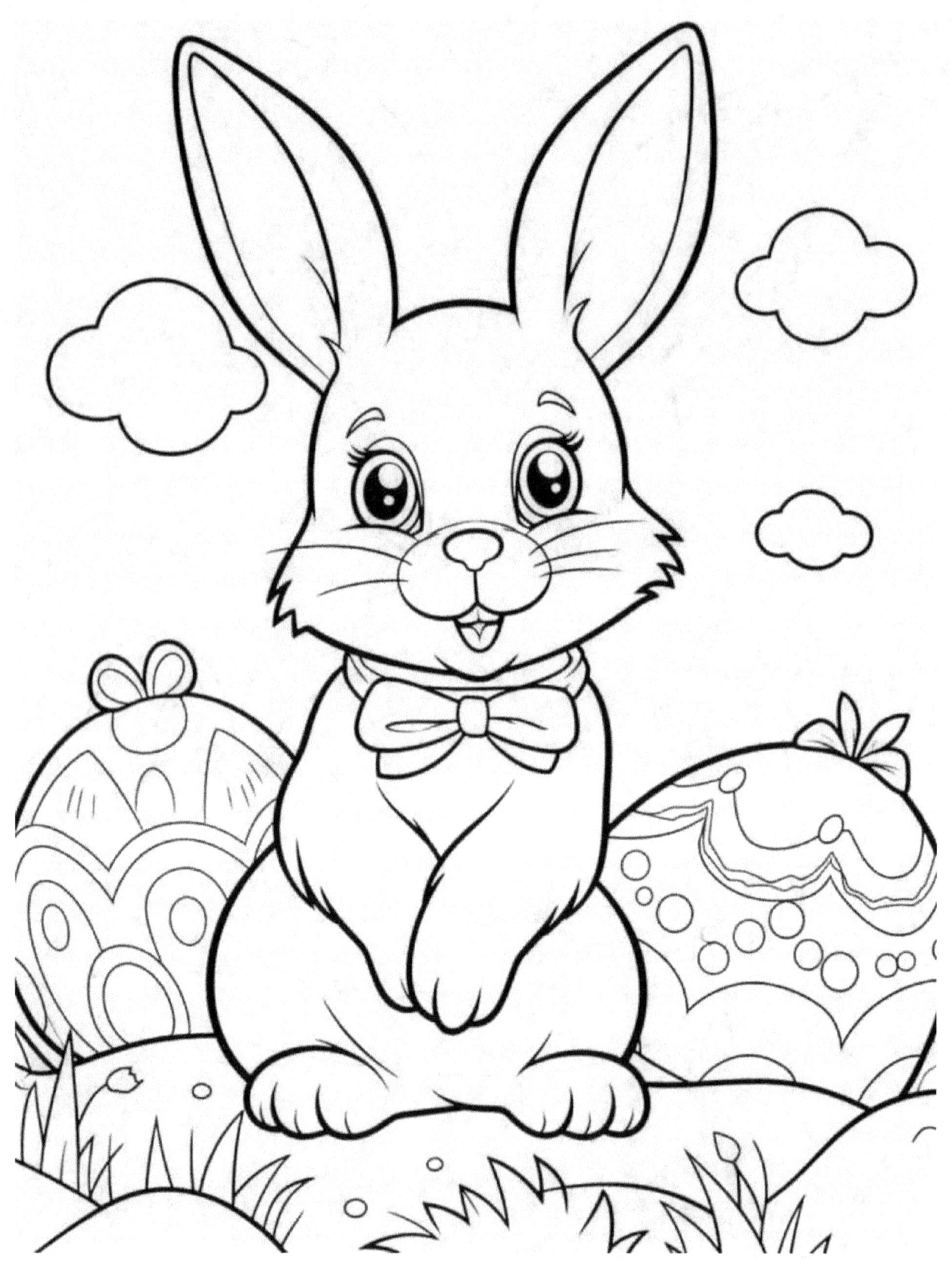

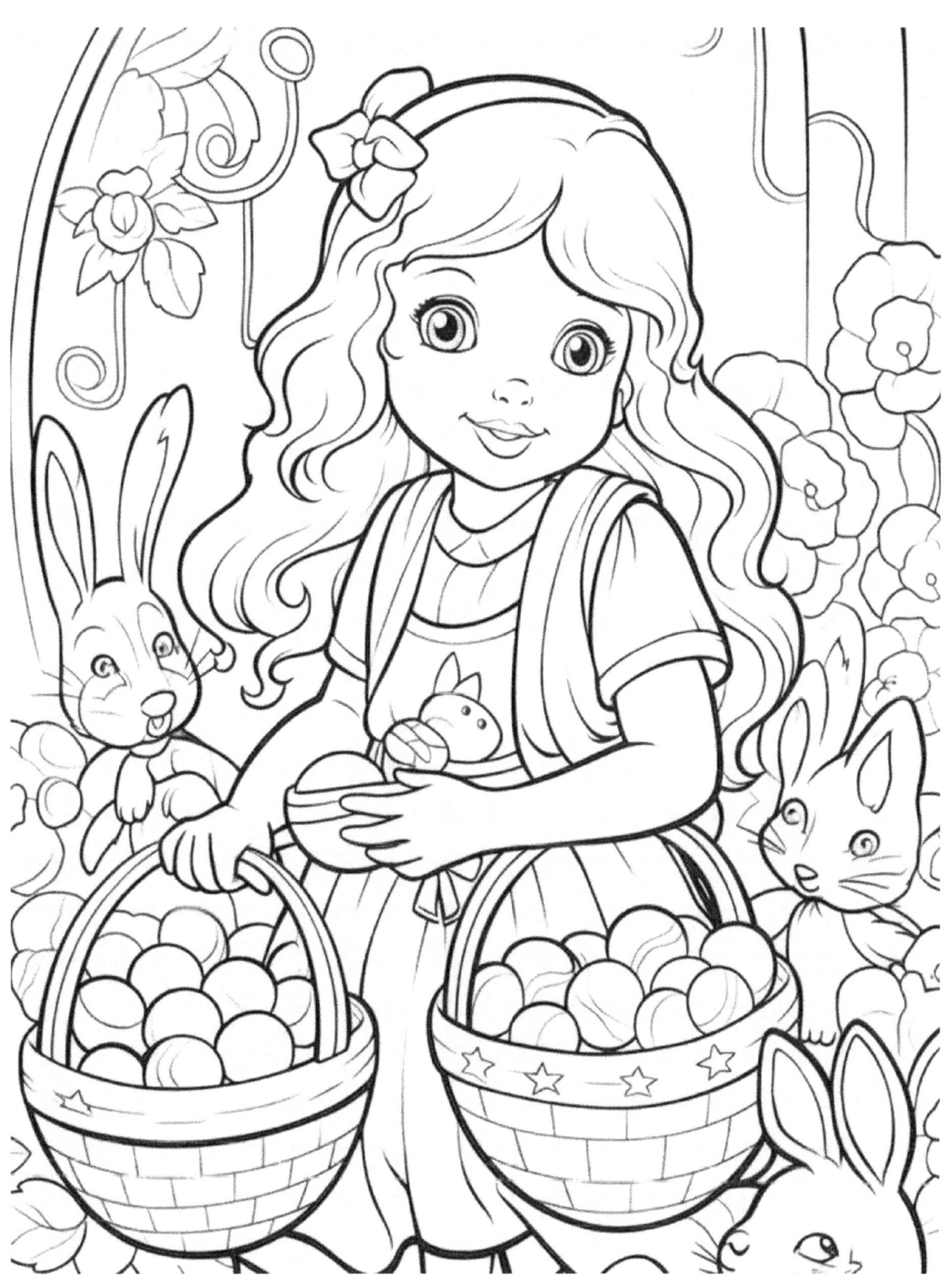

The End

if you liked this book, we have more, scan the QR code

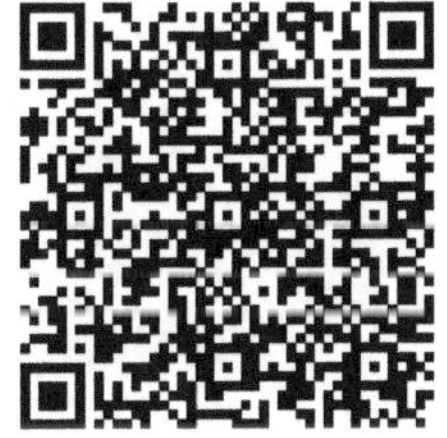